THE
ALLOTMENT
ALMANAC

www.transworldbooks.co.uk

THE
ALLOTMENT
ALMANAC

MONTH-BY-MONTH ON THE PLOT

Terry Walton

BANTAM PRESS

LONDON · TORONTO · SYDNEY · AUCKLAND · JOHANNESBURG

To my two granddaughters Megan and Maisie who have brought so much joy into my already happy life.

Contents

Introduction

WELCOME TO MY HILLSIDE ALLOTMENT in the beautiful Rhondda valley in South Wales!

This precious patch of cultivated ground has been a home from home for me for as long as I can remember. I started at the age of four (I was even born just the other side of the allotment's fence), helping my father look after his crops before being given my own plot when I was eleven. I have been there ever since, hardly missing a day in pursuit of my aim to be completely self-sufficient in fresh, wholesome vegetables and fruit.

I am not alone in my passion. There are forty-two plots on the site, all tended by fellow enthusiasts, some of whom you will meet as you read on. It is a lively as well as a busy place, filled with that strong atmosphere of fellowship and mutual helpfulness that always springs up in a community united in the adventure of growing its own food, especially in the challenging Welsh climate.

There is always something that needs doing, whatever the time of year, but life on an allotment is not all toil. Work is seasoned with plenty of fun and banter, as I describe in the following pages. Whether out on the plot or gathered for coffee in Albie's 'café', the unique spirit of our allotments is one of good humour, support and friendliness, perhaps adding a new angle to 'we'll keep a welcome in the hillside'.

So come with me now and share a typical year on my productive plot on the mountain.

JANUARY

ALONG WITH MANY OTHER GARDENERS, I have little affection for January, usually a thoroughly uninviting month. But shake off the legacy of Christmas excess and home comforts, and (if you look on the bright side) you'll notice the days are lengthening already.

There are even signs that herald spring. In my part of the world, for example, daffodils may well start flowering this month. What a strange but uplifting sight these vibrant blooms can be on a misty morn, lighting up a cold, drab day like little beacons of sunshine.

In my youth (many decades ago!) this was a sight associated more often with March. In fact it could be touch and go some years whether there would be a fully open bloom to wear in the traditional Welsh way on St David's Day. But early flowering of snowdrops and daffodils seems to have grown more commonplace in many areas of the land, another reminder for us of changes to the seasons that are becoming a familiar part of the twenty-first century.

These days I often find myself wondering where winter is hiding. Here in Wales January always used to be very wet and soggy, yet in recent years the month has sometimes been very mild, even positively spring-like when the sun shines. One January, to my surprise, there were definite signs of mating activity in my pond: my frogs had appeared and were doing what usually comes naturally to them in early spring. Clearly it's not just us gardeners, but wildlife too that's becoming confused and 'out of sync' with the calendar!

I now find all too often that my overwintered green manure is far more lush than it should be this early in the season. The rye grass, for example, should be no more than 6 inches (15 cm) high for best value, but after one of these mild winters it can be getting close to double that. Doesn't it know it's still winter? All the prairie animals of the Rhondda might descend on it soon for their late winter grazing!

One year I discovered the chrysanthemums were already sending up strong early shoots, and, to cap it all, greenfly were taking up residence on these tender shoot tips, much to my annoyance. You can't relax for a minute, even in January when you might think everything is still dormant. It was a case of rummaging for my spray to give them a quick unseasonal wash with warm soapy water and put a stop to the aphids' antics before they could do much damage to the new shoots.

Potato plans

Stroll around any garden centre this month and you will see seed potatoes appearing on the shelves. This humble vegetable is worth growing even if you only have a small piece of land or (if really pushed) a few bins or bags.

There is nothing quite like the taste and excitement of harvesting first early potatoes – it's like digging up buried treasure. They might make plenty of green growth on top, but until I lift them there is no clue to what lies beneath. And as those little white beauties hit the light of day, they give me such a thrill: I can hardly wait to get them home to the kitchen and savour the unique flavour of this first of the season's crops.

If you are limited for space, early varieties are the best to grow, as they are out of the soil by June, and that ground can then be used for summer salad crops. On my large allotment I like to stagger harvesting throughout the season by planting earlies, second earlies and maincrops. This ensures a steady supply of potatoes on the plate right through the summer, while the maincrop varieties fill bags for use during the winter months.

Patience is a virtue

There are still plenty of winter crops left for me to harvest – leeks, cabbages, Brussels sprouts and very soon the first curly kale and sprouting broccoli – so we shan't go hungry. But as the month progresses the patience of us gardeners is being tested to the full. I keep looking through all my new seed packets, and the urge to start sowing seems to grow daily.

But hold on a little longer, and the time to start will soon be here. When the gooseberry buds, previously tightly closed, show signs of unfurling, that's the cue to begin outdoors. As long as the preparation work is up to date or under way, a week or two longer will not matter to the life cycle of the crops.

Harvesting the leeks

Tales from the plot

Reflect on this great club that we all belong to, the nationwide community of allotment gardeners: a long-established group of like-minded people that must be over three hundred years old all told. This kind of community gardening started in the eighteenth century when landowners, afraid they might lose their workers to better-paid jobs in the towns, decided the best way to keep them on the land was to give them a plot of ground where they could grow their own food. This supplemented their meagre wages while helping to put wholesome food on their families' tables.

Thus was the allotment created. Plots in those far-off days would have grown a variety of cereal crops as well as vegetables, to provide the family with all their basic requirements. In fact, the only real difference between then and now would be that people today rarely see the need to grow cereals any more, and concentrate instead on a wider variety of vegetables and fruits. The motivation to grow your own produce is somewhat different in the twenty-first century, too. Now, while still fulfilling the object of supplying good, fresh food, it is more of a leisure activity.

If one of those early allotmenteers were to walk through the gates of a modern-day allotment, they would still meet the same type of person as they might have done then: a basically friendly, sharing, happy-go-lucky gardener willing to enthuse about all the benefits of locally grown produce.

Three centuries ago, mind, there were no artificial fertilizers and everyone grew 'organically', except that they would have had little idea what that expression meant. They collected animal manures and compost material as a matter of course, to feed the soil and provide all its rich nourishment. Since the close of the twentieth century, with all its enthusiasm for artificial fertilizers and chemical insecticides, those same old traditions have become the norm again on many plots up and down the land.

The same principles of growing apply today as all those years ago – the practice of crop rotation, for example, which is essential for vigorous and disease-free crops. Gardeners then depended on a system of barter, because money was not yet the major currency of trade for everyone, rich and poor. And this is still true today on the modern allotment, where produce changes hands and surplus crops are likely to be exchanged for those in short supply. In fact, money is not as valuable to any gardener as a bag of fresh vegetables to take home and savour.

So you see, the minute your allotment career starts you are a member of a long-established club. There are no secrets here: knowledge developed and honed over the ages is willingly passed on by older, more experienced allotmenteers, perpetuating these vital skills.

For anyone who is not yet a member of the great allotment movement, think what you might be missing, and make a resolution while the year is still young to get out there and start gardening. I guarantee it will not be long before you are hooked, another life member of this unique club.

It is a sad day in the allotment community when a long-serving member hangs up his boots, but it can also signal an opportunity. When, after many years of gardening on our site, Ronnie decided to give up his plot – a prime position just inside the main gate – one of our existing members was able to move on to this plot with its easier access.

Since the formation of our allotment site nearly a hundred years ago, it has been one of the rules that seniority and good gardening practice are taken into account when allocating prime-location plots. We all started on the high hillside and as the years progress have had the chance to move down gradually to the lower reaches of the site.

This brings a gathering of 'old hands' like me on the lower plots, while the younger, fitter people are concentrated at the top. If you stay long enough and garden well, you have the same opportunity as anyone else to reach utopia on the lower levels. And the gradual shift downwards then creates room for some new allotmenteers on the upper slopes.

When you are a creature of habit as I am and rarely miss a daily trip to the allotments, your absence is soon noticed. My family stayed on a few extra days one New Year, and we were sitting there chatting over a cup of tea when the telephone rang.

'It's for you,' my wife said, handing me the phone. At the other end was Dave H.

'Are you ill?' he asked.

'No, I'm fine,' I replied.

'It's just that we haven't seen you for three days and were wondering where you were,' he explained.

Still, it is good to know that your presence is quickly missed, and Dave's call reawakened the urge to return to my plot.

After a long absence Clive returned briefly to his 'poultry ranch' at the top of the allotments. With all his chickens gone there had been no need for him to make his daily visits until he restocked in the spring. What concerned us mere gardeners on plots below him was that he had a large mound of three-year-old horse manure stacked on his chicken patch, and we kept on casting longing glances at it.

As soon as he turned up we seized the moment. Carl, Brian, Albie and I filled as many bags as we could of the great stuff to spread on our plots. Soon there were over fifty full bags, and thanks mainly to Carl's youth and fitness these were soon carried to our plots. Once we'd all recovered from those exertions we were eagerly awaiting Clive's next visit.

As the great recyclers of the valleys we are always on the lookout for other people's discarded materials.

The other morning Dai arrived at the plot with lots of red trays that were being replaced by the Post Office sorting department. These are very rigid and conveniently hold exactly twenty of the polystyrene cups we all use for growing our plants in, so we did not need much persuasion to take them off his hands. After drilling a few drainage holes in the base, we all have these posh pot holders on display in our greenhouses. One man's waste is our useful free accessory.

During the autumn Brian built a shed the size of a sentry box, tucked away at the bottom of his plot. Recently he decided that it was in the wrong place, so he was looking for some volunteers to help reposition it. With two long poles nailed along its sides to make it easier to lift, it looked exactly like a sedan chair. Dai, Colin, Brian and I were detailed to help in its move, but just as we were all about to lift, I was called away to give out some compost from the communal shed to one of our members.

When I got back, the other three had struggled to move it without my help and were standing there puffing and blowing. I had been there in spirit and had no sympathy with their impatience – if they had only moved it several days earlier they would have had some wind assistance, for it had been blowing a gale. So, it was off to the café for a well-earned coffee. Seeing them so exhausted, I felt as tired as they were.

We do not have many fires on the allotments as the smoke annoys our neighbouring householders, but the other Sunday was an exception. Jeff's old shed, inherited many years ago from Wayne L, was in a parlous, even perilous state and was easier to burn down than demolish.

The locals were duly warned, and quite a crowd gathered at the top of his plot to witness the event and keep warm. It was stuffed with combustible material, a match was struck, and in no time at all it was well alight.

We stood there watching this spectacular blaze like kids at a bonfire party, and even a plot-length away we could feel that warm glow. I only hope the heat spurred his broad beans out of their frozen sleep.

It's not just the plants that change the landscape of the allotments!

Sweetening the soil

It seems just a few short weeks ago that I was bemoaning the fact that my plot was covered by a white blanket of snow. Around now the same thing happens again, this time under my control as I spread a thick layer of white garden lime all over my brassica patch. All the members of the cabbage family (don't forget this includes radish, turnip and swede as well as the more obvious 'greens') easily fall victim to club root, a nasty disfiguring disease made far less severe if the soil is more alkaline. A good coating of lime applied now will reduce the acidity of this patch of ground and make it more congenial for the brassicas.

Liming the brassica patch

Of all the substances that can be added to improve plant performance I find lime one of the most universally beneficial. It is a natural organic mineral that helps the majority of vegetables grow more healthily – particularly peas and beans – so I will be applying it to most other areas on the allotment too, except where potatoes are being grown, as too much lime gives them scab. However, these other areas are not treated just yet as they only need a thin application, and if the next couple of months are wet any benefits could be leached out of the soil.

Help with pest control

After a good autumn, when there is plenty of food in the hedgerows and surrounding countryside, my plot can be a silent place without the activity of those winter birds that normally grace my multitude of feeders. There are always a few regulars such as blue tits, bullfinches and, of course, my cheeky resident robin, but the rest are missing. I still constantly top up their feeders when required, but the rate at which they empty is much slower than normal.

You might argue that foraging in the wild is more natural for these birds and that the money in my pocket goes a little further in these austere times, but I reckon we need the help of those birds nonetheless. I am of course talking about the gardener's top pests: slugs and snails. Even this early in the year they'll be tucking into the greenery of my sprout plants and enjoying the fresh delicate leaves of my spring cabbage. They never seem to go elsewhere on a long winter sabbatical or disappear into the lower reaches of my soil.

To me a slug is a slug and they all behave the same, but apparently there are thirty different species of them (some are even 'goodies' that eat the others), and – worse still – ninety species of snail roaming our gardens.

They can make an impressive mess of a row of seedlings in a short space of time, and no wonder: unlike us with our handful of teeth, each of these pests has upwards of 20,000 teeth in its restless maw. And each can become the grandparent to 90,000 grandchildren! It's easy to see how they can soon rule the roost in any garden if left unchecked.

The ways of controlling these night-time (usually) marauders are many, but in my view none has proved effectual at totally eliminating these monsters. As I am an organic gardener the task becomes even harder. Blue slug pellets are effective, but they can be detrimental to other wildlife when they enter the food chain. Barriers work when it is dry, but the minute they get wet slugs slither over them unharmed. I am in my second trial year of using nematodes – a predator – and I'm hoping this natural form of attack could reduce the problem, although the nematodes only work when the soil is warm enough and while there are still slugs and snails around.

Hence my efforts to attract birds. We might hate those nibbling molluscs but they and their eggs do have a significant role in the food chain, providing fresh meat for thrushes and blackbirds and, in the case of the tiny ones, a meal for the robin. Until the birds return from the wild, though, my only recourse is vigilance and night-time patrols, armed with a flashlight and a sharp knife.

Stealing a march on nature

Early crops started now are essential in helping to plug the 'hungry gap' in a few weeks' time, the moment when existing vegetables are coming to an end and there's nothing fresh ready to replace them. Any crops in store are beginning their new life cycle – potatoes are starting to sprout and the onions are sending out green shoots as they start growing again. How are we dedicated gardeners going to manage without our daily 'dose' of home-grown vegetables?

This is where the earliest sowings in the greenhouse come into play. We can grow these on under the protection of the glass and they will thrive, given a little added warmth from whatever form of heating you apply to your greenhouse. When gradually hardened off and planted under cloches, they will provide fresh food in late April.

Lettuce and cabbage mature very well under this method and supply the very first tasty vegetables of a new season. Use the heated greenhouse to get an early crop of new potatoes, too – plant some in a large drum in one corner and you could be savouring new potatoes on your plate during May.

Seed potatoes in a container are topped up with compost when shoots poke through

Airing-cupboard culture

On our cold, wet hillside in the Rhondda I would never dare to sow broad beans out on the patch in November: every slug and bird would have a field day. As January progresses I like to have them coming along indoors, together with early transplants of 'Primo' cabbage, butterhead lettuces and onion seedlings, well settled into their compartmented seed trays.

If you don't have a greenhouse, a warm windowsill or even a cold frame will allow you to get these crops going. I like to start my broad beans by chitting them in sealed freezer bags. I spray some multi-purpose compost with water in a mixing tray until it just about clings together like a snowball. Then I fill the freezer bag with this moistened compost, pour in the seeds from the packet, and mix it all well together so all the seeds are in contact with the compost. After three to four days in the warm airing cupboard, little white roots should have started to appear, and I immediately take the germinating seeds out for potting up.

Chitted broad beans

Onion seeds also need sowing now to give them the long growing season they require. They go into the airing cupboard to germinate in warmth, while the landing windowsill houses trays of early lettuce and cabbage. My wife is always alarmed at my takeover of parts of the house as a giant propagator, but with outside temperatures on the rise I'll soon be moving the seed trays out to the greenhouse.

She knows I'll be back in the airing cupboard again, though, when it is time to sow my tomatoes and cucumbers. Oh, the patience of a gardener's wife!

Home-made materials

I mix my own compost for potting on or pricking out all these indoor sowings, using a good multi-purpose brand as a base. To this I add twenty-five per cent by volume of worm compost from my wormery and then have the perfect medium for encouraging strong, sturdy plants right up until they are ready to go out in the ground at the end of March. As further encouragement they are potted up in used polystyrene cups, which I collect from local factories and offices. With a couple of holes burned in the bottom using a screwdriver heated in the flame of Albie's greenhouse stove, these make the perfect warm accommodation for the early seedlings.

Heated salads

While there is warmth on offer in the mini plastic greenhouse inside my greenhouse, it seems a pity not to make use of it, so I sow a pot of basil for an early hint of summer. This is joined by a pot of salad-leaf or 'cut-and-come-again' lettuce. When this pops through, the pot finds a home on our kitchen windowsill, where we can harvest the tiny leaves with a pair of scissors regularly whenever required. With care they will keep on supplying cuts of leaves for several weeks.

Covering up rhubarb

Rhubarb – a vegetable that you either love or loathe. This vegetable (or maybe a fruit, an argument we could debate for hours) has been the backbone of gardening for centuries. It was commonplace on every allotment during my youth, but then fell from grace for some reason. Now – partly thanks to the influence of some television chefs and their culinary skills – it is making a comeback. And not before time.

Me? I have always grown it and loved it, particularly when young and forced. If you want these tender, pale pink stalks, now is the time to take action. The Victorians had their very fancy earthenware pots to cover the crowns and force the stalks in darkness, but I just use an old plastic dustbin – not quite as attractive as those antique clay pots, but nonetheless a very effective way of producing long, juicy, tasty stalks.

Place the bin over a large crown as its fat buds are emerging, and weigh it down with a couple of large stones to prevent it being blown away in the winter gales. Check on progress regularly by peeking under the bin – you'll be surprised how quickly the stems grow in this cosy dark microclimate. Come early March, you could be savouring the flavour of delicious rhubarb crumble and custard. Now there's a mouth-watering prospect!

New rhubarb stalks

Making a rhubarb bed

This is my favourite month for starting another bed for rhubarb. In the early autumn I dig up some of my old crowns and chop them in pieces with a spade. I discard the older parts, keeping young pieces with a good bud on top. I leave these youngsters on the surface of the soil for (hopefully) a few good doses of frost, which causes the bud to remain dormant and build up strength while it is resting.

Around now I prepare the new bed with copious amounts of well-rotted manure, and then plant the rested divisions with just the tips of their buds above the surface. This is all you need to do to bring forth a bumper crop of rhubarb stalks to grace your dessert dishes for most of the summer.

Go on, give it a go. If you've never tasted fresh home-grown rhubarb, you are in for a treat. Who knows, you may love it as much as I do.

Digging deep for peas

On a good day this month there is one particular task that I must complete. If I am to get a crop of sweet-smelling, vibrant-coloured sweet peas to enhance summer evenings on the allotment, I need to prepare a trench for them.

My method is to open up a trench approximately 20 inches (50 cm) deep and fill the base of this with the contents of my summer pots and hanging baskets. In addition to my own supply, many of my neighbours see me as a way to recycle their green waste, and by the time I have finished the trench is usually lined to a depth of some 10 inches (25 cm).

I cover all this green waste and old potting compost with about 6 inches (15 cm) of well-rotted manure. Then the trench is left exposed to the elements for a month before being filled up with soil.

I now have the ideal preparation for my abundant crop of sweet peas, and they love the rich, moisture-retentive nature of their summer home. All that is left to do is to sow the seeds in my greenhouse at the end of this month – three seeds per 3-inch (8 cm) pot – and by the end of April their new home will be perfect, waiting to receive them, and they'll be eager to move in.

Drumming up root crops

Recycling other people's waste, partly to save money but chiefly with the objective of producing good wholesome food, is central to my philosophy.

Recently I came into possession of two 45-gallon (200-litre) plastic water butts. As I already have a series of these dotted around the plot to provide water for my thirsty crops in the height of summer (well, perhaps not during the past three or four years), I've taken these extra drums and drilled some 1-inch (2.5 cm) holes in the bottom for drainage.

Part-filled with a layer of my own compost and then topped up with the contents of a growbag or two, they make the perfect home for some carrots and parsnips. The drums just need to be left for about two weeks for the contents to settle, and then they are wrapped up in some bubble polythene to help warm them up in time for sowing those long-rooted vegetables early next month.

Try flower sprouts

I love the challenge of trying new varieties of vegetables. Most have been in seed catalogues for many years, though not grown by me, but occasionally a completely novel vegetable turns up, which adds to the excitement of experimenting and tasting something new.

A recent newcomer being grown for a particular supermarket (sold as 'flower sprouts') and now available to us gardeners is the leafy sprout. This grows in the same way as normal Brussels sprouts but instead of producing tight buttons bears mini-cabbages, something gardeners have tried for years to prevent on conventional plants – a condition technically known as being 'blown' and usually a sign of soil that is too loose.

Give bees a hand

Some reports suggest the bee population has declined by as much as fifty per cent in recent years. Like many gardeners I am passionate about these insects, and this is bad news for anyone who is keen on growing fruit and vegetables.

One way to encourage bees is to grow plants that provide plenty of the nectar needed by these hard-working creatures. Growing some especially nectar-rich flowers alongside and between our blander vegetables will help these insects flourish, and they will 'reward' us by pollinating the blossoms of our precious fruiting crops. Without the unseen work that these friends perform we would all suffer a lack of good harvests.

Nature usually has a way of adapting and surviving, but sometimes it needs a hand from us. Growing the flowers bees like, such as poached-egg plant (*Limnanthes douglasii*), combined with sensible gardening and a reduction in our dependence on insecticides can bring about the changes needed and start to restore the delicate balances of our environment.

The new sprout variety – actually a sprout crossed with curly kale and christened 'Petit Posy' or 'Brukale' – is cunningly designed to fool children into eating these nutritious vegetables, because these have a sweeter, milder flavour than normal kinds, and look prettier on the plate. We'll wait and see if this is indeed the case.

But meanwhile I shall get hold of some of these seeds and be the first to grow them on our allotments. That should fool some of the more diehard gardeners!

Home-grown manure

With spring just around the corner, it's time to say goodbye to my 'green, green grass of home'.

For the past six years my winter gardening routine has changed significantly. Before that I had always been a traditional allotment keeper, turning all the vacant ground on my plot into large clods with a spade during the autumn, leaving it rough for the elements to do their job of breaking it down into a fine tilth over the winter. Climate change has completely upset that routine, however, because winters have generally become wetter and all this extra rainfall dissolves the stored nutrients and leaches them from the soil.

To combat this I now sow rye grass at the beginning of September, and the lush green topgrowth of this carpets any vacant ground throughout the ravages of the winter's rains. The fibrous root structure it produces clings on to the nutrients that might otherwise have been lost. Between now and the end of February I turn this growth back into the soil as 'green manure', making our neighbourhood horse almost redundant.

Green manure carpeting the plot

Last year, for the first time, I mixed the rye grass with vetches. These have little white nitrogen-fixing nodules clearly visible on the roots and so help reinforce the nutrient value of the green manure. I have hopefully reached the almost perfect blend for enriching my soil with a combination of 'lifters' and 'fixers' – the green rye grass lifting the humus level of the soil while the vetches fix that vital element, nitrogen.

I do not rely on this green manure alone to give my soil added oomph, however. Before digging it in I spread a rich coating of well-rotted horse manure over the top of it, plus a garnish of a few bags of pigeon manure that has been weathered well. The finished areas are then nigh on perfect for those greedy crops of potatoes, onions, leeks and beans.

Cheat a little outdoors

When January has nearly expired it is time to plan and think of those first sowings outdoors, and to devise ways of cheating on nature. Many people cover areas of their ground with black sheeting or old carpet to warm the soil a few degrees. This does the job well while in place, but the temperature will fall again once the protection is removed.

The best way to warm a small patch of soil – enough to sow a few seeds – is to place a cloche over it. Polythene used to be the favoured covering for cloches, but this can sweat with condensation, and eventually the ground beneath dries out. It seems an unnecessary chore to have to keep on removing the polythene to water the early sowings housed below.

I find by far the best cover for cloches is horticultural fleece or, for anyone with a bigger budget, a thicker but similar material called Enviromesh. These allow the ground and plants to breathe, while any gentle rain that falls passes straight through. This is the perfect environment for early sowings of carrots, lettuce and cabbage during the next few weeks, protecting them from the elements and maintaining the soil temperature a few degrees warmer than the surroundings.

JANUARY IN A NUTSHELL

Key jobs for JANUARY

- ✔ Keep harvesting winter vegetables.
- ✔ Cover rhubarb for an early blanched crop.
- ✔ Prepare sweet-pea trench.
- ✔ Sow sweet-pea seeds indoors.
- ✔ Lime brassica area.
- ✔ Sow broad beans indoors.
- ✔ Sow onion seeds indoors.

If you have time . . .

- ✔ Sow a pot of basil.
- ✔ Sow a pot of cut-and-come-again lettuce.

Looking ahead to FEBRUARY

- ✔ Sow tomatoes.
- ✔ Sow early carrots in a container in the greenhouse.
- ✔ Plant shallots.
- ✔ Prepare greenhouse border for early sowings of salads.

The allotment in winter

Thought for the month

We never know at this time of year what Mother Nature has in store for us come the spring and summer, but one thing always looks likely: food prices will be still higher.

This is the moment for all gardeners (and those who are not!) to resolve to do something about it. Everyone who has an allotment can supplement the household budget by using the ground more productively, cramming sowings of catch crops in between slow-maturing vegetables. Try filling in the spaces between Brussels sprout plants with some fast-growing salad crops, which will be in and out of the soil before the sprouts realize it. If you are growing sweetcorn, let a few climbing French beans use the corn stems as canes and get two harvests from the single patch.

Anyone who at present only grows flowers can plant some vegetables in amongst them. A few carrots, some beetroot and the pretty leaves of cut-and-come-again lettuce will not detract from the beauty of the borders and can all add tasty morsels to your plate. I'd even suggest it might be time to sacrifice some of that pristine lawn and build a raised bed there instead. A few simple, interlocking plastic boards will soon make a useful vegetable patch. And those with no garden at all? Well, any space will do, and just a few pots filled with compost can support a selection of favourite vegetables.

Everyone can join the gardening revolution and have home-grown crops to savour this summer. Who knows, you may get the bug, expand your growing enterprise and before long be on the road to self-sufficiency.

FEBRUARY

OUT ON THE PLOT IT IS STILL TIME to sit on your hands and be patient. February is renowned for having a sting in its tail, and most years the soil is still far too cold to go ahead with new crops. The season is yet young, with plenty of time for sowing and planting.

For all its reputation, February can offer hints of the weeks to come. Only the other year, for example, I returned from the plot at lunchtime, made sandwiches and coffee, and took them out to the patio. Sitting in the warm sunshine and eating my lunch, I looked around me. Gorgeous winter pansies were in full bloom, filling my patio pots with their vibrant deep purples, sunny yellows and rich pink colours, and I was amazed to see honey bees flitting amongst their flowers collecting pollen. I closed my eyes, and could almost believe my life had moved on several months to June.

Even though the year is only in its second month, it will not be long before the garden is a show of bright colours, fruit blossom and vigorous young vegetables, the air filled with beautiful scents and lively sounds. And the thought came to mind that we gardeners are very lucky that we can experience all this life at first hand, savouring the perfume of scented flowers and the more down-to-earth smell of damp soil, or testing the firmness of swelling vegetables. To my mind nothing is more satisfying than popping early pea pods and tasting those very first crisp, juicy peas straight from the pod.

One of the beauties of gardening is that it raises and accentuates all our sensory abilities to their highest level.

WHAT TO LOOK OUT FOR THIS MONTH

The weather often dominates life on the plot more than usual in February. In my experience the ground can be frozen hard and life at a standstill, or it may be so mild that the first frogspawn appears in the pond and the nights are given over to the activity of amorous frogs. The trouble is that a cold snap can suddenly curtail their nocturnal frolics, sending them back to their winter hideaways to await warmer nights. It is not only gardeners who might be kept guessing what season it is this month.

Rusty leeks

If winter has been really wet my February patrols will often reveal an outbreak of rust speckling the outer leaves of the remaining leeks. They need using up fast, although most of those left are smaller than average and will soon be cleared.

It is a good idea to dig up any left-over leeks at the end of this month for temporary heeling in elsewhere, to free up the bed for the next crop. While I'm at it I like to prepare the new home for this year's batch of these versatile vegetables. Once their bed is marked out, given there is plenty of well-rotted manure on my heap, the wheelbarrow comes out to dump a good coating on the surface. It's good warming work on a cold morning. Then when I need my next exercise session I'll spread the manure and dig it in.

Extra-early potatoes

There are always welcome finds to be had on the plot when doing certain jobs, even at this time of year. The other week I was emptying my pair of half-drums, which last year housed some maincrop potatoes, followed by a planting of late salad vegetables. While clearing out the contents on to the soil I came across some potatoes left buried deep in this rich compost despite my attempts to harvest them all before sowing the salads. They were still good, just like new potatoes, and made a fine meal on my dinner plate. I was thankful the winter had been mild or the tubers might have been frozen to mush in the drums (metal is a good conductor of cold as well as heat) and this lucky meal would have been lost.

Hokey Cokey shallots

They say curiosity killed the cat, but there's nothing quite so inquisitive as a foraging blackbird. Anything that looks remotely edible or simply interesting is at its mercy. One year I had barely finished planting my shallots nice and early when, first thing next morning, I found many of them lying on the surface of the soil. My resident blackbird had plucked them up, believing they were worms. All was not rosy on the Walton plot.

I quickly replanted the bulbs, this time hiding their tips just below the surface where I thought they were safely out of sight, but next day some had been pulled up yet again. I forget what variety they were, but I rechristened them Hokey Cokey shallots as the batch seemed to be forever in, out and shaken all about. So watch out for that prowling blackbird this month if you have planted shallots or onion sets already.

A gardener's devotion

You need to keep an eye on conditions under glass this month. Sometimes it can be freezing, almost as cold as outside. Next moment the warmth of the late morning sun can make it feel positively tropical, which has a great impact on the seeds sown under cover. They germinate fast and, once they have emerged, can grow on at an alarming rate. This means much more pricking out to do, sometimes overwhelming the available space with full seed trays. Then, of course, comes early evening, and with it a rapid drop in temperature. So I have to cluster the trays all round the paraffin lamp to keep them cosy and frost-free.

They are like my little children and I am sure, given time, they would all have names.

Seed trays keeping cosy around the lamp

Tales from the plot

Tending a plot has its ups and downs. There was an air of gloom on Dave H's plot the other week, for example, when he emerged from his greenhouse shaken and devastated. He had chitted his broad beans and then planted the germinating seeds into individual pots. Almost overnight he was horrified to discover that his resident mouse had held a party with its mates, and had dug up and devoured all but seven of his precious crop. So it was back to square one for poor old Dave, as is so often the way in gardening. He was lucky in this instance, though – with it being only February, there was still time to catch up.

On our allotment we have a store shed that caters for all the members' needs. In recent years some of us have turned to organic methods, relying heavily on manure and compost rather than chemical feeds to increase the fertility of the soil, and for us the store sells blood, fish and bone, a traditional mixture that is the backbone (excuse the pun) of the organic feeding regime.

Other members prefer to use chemical fertilizers to achieve their goal – there's no rigid policy imposed on our site – and for them the store sells sulphate of ammonia, superphosphate, sulphate of potash and the general fertilizer Growmore. At some time in our gardening career all we older gardeners have probably used a combination of these various fertilizers, together with manure, to achieve our goals. There is no doubt in my mind that chemical fertilizers do give spectacular results. A feed of nitrogen will give onions and brassicas a growth spurt, making them look dark green and healthy. Sulphate of potash helps fruiting crops successfully set fruit, and superphosphate improves the growth of the pea and bean family. This is instant food with almost instant visible results.

But for me that is where it ends. We all like our crops to look appealing but to me the secret lies in their taste on the plate.

Chemically fed crops grow so rapidly they have no time to capture the subtler flavours developed by slowly absorbing natural minerals and nutrients from the soil. These flavours are present in soil that has built up a mass of micro-organisms feeding on the natural materials added over a long period.

This slow but sure fertility remains, whereas excessive rain leaches chemicals from the soil. It might take time and effort to grow crops organically, but the rewards more than compensate for this. It is this move back (it's nothing new!) to basic organic growing that has brought people back to the allotments, knowing they can take charge of what they grow and that it will be safe and flavoursome.

Ultimately what you grow and how you grow it is your choice, of course, but having lived by both methods I know which I prefer. Yes, I am a total organic nut!

It is strange how confusion about green potatoes lingers. One of our more recent members bought some seed potatoes from the store shed one day. Two weeks later I was standing in there when he brought them back, complaining they had gone green.

'They're poisonous,' he said accusingly.

'I thought you were going to plant them,' I replied mildly.

'I was!'

'Then there's no problem,' I reassured him. 'They are only poisonous if you eat them.'

Any potato will turn green in light, it's a natural process, and then they are not fit to eat. But they are perfectly safe to plant.

Remember, always keep potatoes in a dark place or bag if you're storing them to eat, and never leave them exposed to daylight. Even gardening can be dangerous if you don't follow the rules.

While I was working in the store one day, two strangers arrived at the gate and politely asked where Bob's plot was. Under their arms they carried a roll of cushion flooring that you would normally expect to find adorning a kitchen floor. Armed with a few simple instructions they set off along the path to find his little plot. At the time, although a little inquisitive, I was very busy, so I didn't try to find out the purpose of this delivery.

The following morning I was still tidying the store when the gate opened and the same two blokes entered, this time carrying a roll of carpet. Off they went, knowing the way and not needing any directions, and about half an hour later they left empty-handed. At last I could not contain my curiosity any longer and I wandered over to Bob's plot. There, sitting resplendent in his newly carpeted shed, was Bob himself, his double-glazed entrance 'hall' neatly covered with cushion flooring. I was instructed to slip off my muddy wellies outside on the path before daring to enter his now palatial shed.

In my youth there were no sheds or greenhouses on any of our plots, each of which was conscientiously tended in exactly the same manner. In those days our allotment committee had strict rules for how a plot should be looked after and these were slavishly followed. A path 18 inches (45 cm) wide surrounded every plot and the whole enclosed area was filled with crops of almost the same nature. Paths had to be kept clean, with no overhanging fruit bushes, and the plot was to be cultivated fully and used exclusively for growing produce.

But the years have rolled on, and inevitably habits and attitudes have changed. The landscape greatly altered as greenhouses and sheds sprang up on every plot – not pristine purchased dwellings, you realize, but ramshackle creations put together from discarded materials and the gleanings of skips. As these unique buildings began to grace every plot the allotments evolved into a charming shanty town, every structure an insight and testimony to the plot-holder's character and DIY skill. Those old committee members wouldn't recognize the place!

A further development, once people had a little more money in their pockets, was the gradual change of emphasis from plots for crops to the allotment as a leisure area. First a small pond would appear as everyone realized water wasn't out of place on the plot, and that leaving frogs to control slugs was much kinder to the environment than scattering little blue pellets. A band of grass might surround the pond, providing space for a bench as a place to sit and meditate while the crops grew away silently. Soon plots were being subdivided into individual areas, with metal sheets creating small patches to house each crop – and the raised bed was born. With them came more paths, running in all directions across the plot.

Me? I am still a traditionalist, with just one path and a large plot swelling with all those bountiful crops in season. I am sure that if those old committee men are looking down they might be disturbed by all these radical changes in gardening style. But change is a fact of life and everyone has to accept that eventually. Gardening is forever evolving; the uniqueness of every plot makes for variety and creates a place where your character shines through. Personally I am all for it.

It is a great sight to see Gary with his son and grandson, all working on his plot together. I remember my days as a child, helping my father on his plot and happily getting my hands dirty without a ticking off from my mother. I enjoyed the experience so much that it has stuck with me ever since. It is at this early age that the seeds of a life of gardening are sown, growing into a passion that can remain with you always. Allotments are not just for adults; after all, most of us 'old-timers' started there while young. Far from being a serious, grown-up kind of place, allotments are there for families to enjoy themselves, spend quality time together, and – who knows? – perhaps start a new way of life for someone.

PLOT PROGRESS

Much of the plot is in a kind of transition this month as the overwintered crops are used up and the ground is still in a state of preparation for the new season. As always much depends on the weather. 'February Fill-dyke' is an old-fashioned name that reflects the amount of rain we used to get around now, but some years recently there has been an unusual spell of warm dry weather this month, leaving the ground in perfect condition for preparing the various beds. Sometimes I have even managed to get my shallots planted out into the onion bed and carefully hidden away from the eyes of preying birds.

Too much progress indoors

It only takes a few days of unbroken February sunshine to lift the temperature in the greenhouse into the mid-30s Celsius, producing subtropical conditions by the early afternoon. The seedlings safely housed there respond very quickly to these unusual conditions, leaping ahead of their growth schedule and overcrowding the staging.

Broad beans can be bouncing out of their pots, closely followed by the sweet peas, so I have to ventilate freely to hold them back. Early lettuce and cabbage appear within days in these conditions, chivvying

Early cabbage and lettuce seedlings

me into pricking them out in more spacious modular seed trays so they can grow on unchecked into sturdy plants, ready for planting out under cloches in March. All this unseasonal rate of growth stimulated by an unusually warm early February.

The other extreme

Out on the plots severe nightly frosts and a covering of snow should have attacked those large clods of soil left exposed by my traditionalist neighbours' regime of winter digging, and by now these will have started the process of crumbling into fine particles of soil – nature's way of preparing a patch for those not so far distant sowings. On my own plot the green manure crop will be ready to be turned into the soil – if January has not already supplied the opportunity. The remains of my winter vegetables usually look rather sad after withstanding the rigours of an extremely cold winter, but can still provide feasts in my winter soups and hot dinners, and are often all the sweeter for those unseen actions of frost in converting starches to sugars.

There may not be much in the way of 'prettiness' about a February plot, but the cold frosty nights are exactly what is needed to bring a respite to all my dormant fruit bushes, forcing them to rest before they bring forth spring bud burst and blossom for all those luscious summer fruits.

Much to do

Although we can sneak up on Mother Nature and get ahead of the game by sowing early in a greenhouse, there is plenty to do out on the plot and very often at least a handful of days when we can get on with it.

In an average year snow should have gone by now and, with the soil gently warming up, crops like overwintered onions and autumn-planted garlic soon make a visible spurt of growth. I like to get in there early and loosen the soil between the plants with the Dutch hoe. This will prevent

Garlic emerging from wet soil

the early weeds taking hold and allow the soil to breathe a little, always a relief for the crop if heavy winter rains have battered the surface.

The plastic covering can come off my old manure heap, workable again now after being frozen for some weeks, so it is time to get that squeaky old wheelbarrow back into service. I use some broken canes to mark out my onion bed and my broad bean and potato areas, and liberally cover these with barrowloads of this 'black gold'. Spread really thickly this will help retain plenty of moisture and goodness in the ground for these demanding crops. If the weather turns bad, at least the carting is done ready for my digging sessions; if it stays fair I turn the manure, brown and green, in while the ground is workable and let it all blend together to produce rich arable spots for these greedy feeders.

If I am lucky and have done the job well, I'll be reaping the rewards for the rest of the year.

IN THE GREENHOUSE

More perhaps than any other month of the year, February is a time to be busy in the greenhouse, where the new season is already well under way. The space under glass fills rapidly, with more crops being sown day by day. Eventually this puts pressure on me to restore the wormery to its place of glory outdoors on the plot, but not before removing yet another tray of fine compost after these busy little worms have been munching non-stop. The warmth of the greenhouse keeps them active during cold spells and the reward is tray after tray of waste material converted into one of the best planting media.

One out, two in

The space made vacant by this timely eviction allows me to bring in a large tub that used to house my granddaughter's toys. This is where I plant the first of my early potatoes. A good helping of well-rotted horse manure goes in the bottom, covered with 5 inches (13 cm) of growbag compost. On this I plant five 'Winston' first early potato tubers, equally spaced out and then covered with 4 inches (10 cm) of the growbag mix.

A jacket of bubble wrap around the tub, a slight soaking, then I pop them in a corner and forget about them for a week or two. It's important to leave space above the surface in the tub for adding more compost as the shoots appear, and to continue reburying them until the tub is full: this is the same process as earthing up potatoes outdoors, but a lot easier. All being well there will be a bountiful supply of bright new tubers in early June.

While I'm at it, I bring inside another small blue bin and fill it with good compost. This is sown with an early batch of stump-rooted carrots. I make a spiral drill from the centre of the drum outwards using my finger, then sow the seeds thinly and sieve a little of the compost over them. Finally I water them lightly, cover the bin with bubble wrap to retain the moisture, keep it all warm in the greenhouse, and wait.

Home-made gadgets

While transplanting some seedlings recently I realized I was using the same gadget that was first made for me over forty years ago. It is a piece of Bakelite (any old-timers like me will recall this was the tough plastic material wirelesses – sorry, radios – and telephones were manufactured from), about half an inch (13 mm) wide and 8 inches (20 cm) long. One end is ground flat to ease a seedling from the compost, the other rounded to make the perfect hole into which to drop it.

I was a young man working through my apprenticeship when an older, skilled man discovered my passion for gardening and made this useful tool for me. I have treasured this unique tool all my gardening life since and must have transplanted tens of thousands of seedlings with it, yet it still looks good as new. It is true, they don't make things like they used to.

I also have a piece of square board to the centre of which is nailed an old wooden spade handle. The same width as a seed tray, the board is perfect for firming the compost down before sowing seeds. How many readers of this book, I wonder, have some similarly special or quirky home-made tool designed to make gardening life simpler? They say gardeners have the perfect answer for making light work of any gardening job.

Starting tomatoes

For anyone with the benefit of a greenhouse, no matter how small, now is a good time to start off some tomatoes. They need some gentle heat to get them under way, plus a little care at first while the season is young, but they are actually a lot hardier than we give them credit for. Have you noticed in the beer gardens of pubs that sell food there are often little clumps of germinating seedlings in a corner wherever someone has cast aside a piece of tomato?

Glance through any seed catalogue these days and there seem to be dozens of novel tomato varieties of all colours and shapes. You can buy tumbling kinds to grow in a hanging basket, or large beefsteak varieties that fill your hand with a single fruit and give that true Mediterranean experience (why is it that when I grow these they always turn out looking grotesque?). Call me conservative but I stick to what I know will do well, and prefer to grow 'Shirley', 'Ferline' and those bite-size beauties 'Gardener's Delight' – I could not do without a handful of ripe cherry tomatoes to satisfy my mid-morning hunger in the summertime.

Try your own peppers

Late February is a good time for greenhouse owners with a little heat to make an early sowing of some pepper seeds: they seem to take an age to produce those green, orange and red fruits, and a start now is ideal. Use a 5-inch (13 cm) pot for these early sowings; sprinkle the seeds thinly on the surface of some sieved multi-purpose compost and then cover them lightly with the same sifted mix. They need warm conditions to germinate, so the

Sowing peppers

pots can be kept in a propagator or (as is my habit) in the airing cupboard back home. Check them daily in case they germinate quickly, to make sure they do not get leggy – as soon as the first shoots are through they need moving into good light. Pot them on into individual 6-inch (15 cm) pots and they should be ready for the greenhouse border in April or May.

Push ahead with pricking out

Late January sowings of lettuce and cabbage usually start to show their first true leaves three to four weeks later, an indication that they want a place of their own far from the crowded seed tray. This is the moment when I transplant them into trays with separate compartments ('modules' or 'cell trays') so that they can grow on into decent-sized plants without competition from their neighbours.

Onion seedlings, too, are often well advanced by now, though still bent over in their looped or 'hairpin' phase, the perfect time to transplant them singly into modules. I use plastic seed-tray inserts divided into twenty-four (six × four) individual cells, filled with fresh multi-purpose compost. Although it is a bit late in the season if you want to match those giant onions on the show bench, these seedlings will still give me the kind of large bulbs I need by the end of the summer. As an insurance I supplement my onion stock by planting some sets, but these are still in my shed waiting for next month.

Early salads and catch crops for borders

I like to have my greenhouse borders ready for this summer's tomatoes by now, and it seems a waste not to use the prepared space for a little early cropping. So I sow a few short rows of radishes, wild rocket, spring onions and (against all the rules about manured ground) an early carrot variety to force for some baby roots. These are covered with some plastic cloches for additional protection and will hopefully supply a few early harvests well before the tomatoes are ready to fill the borders.

My first main sowing of spring onions goes in now, too, using 'White Lisbon', which for me is the perfect salad onion with a season-long harvest of green tops and perfectly white shanks. The container I like to grow them in is the kind of bucket used by florists to display flowers – with a few holes drilled in the base, these are ideal. I start with about 5 inches (13 cm) of well-rotted manure in the base to feed these greedy plants, then I fill the rest of the bucket with good multi-purpose compost, sprinkle the seeds sparsely on the surface and finally cover them with half an inch (13 mm) of the same compost.

Watered gently with a spray of tepid water, they are then popped under the greenhouse staging until they germinate (they should appear after about three weeks). The secret of ensuring a steady sequence of these delicious onions is to sow in succession every three to four weeks so that the supply never runs dry. Grown indoors like this, the first sowing should be ready to harvest in twelve weeks' time.

Wild rocket with its slightly peppery taste adds spice to the salad bowl. If I grow it in a container, I find a pot about 9 inches (23 cm) in diameter is big enough to house this sowing, with the seeds sprinkled sparingly on the surface and covered with a thin layer of compost. Like the onions, these are lightly watered and tucked under the bench, where seedlings should appear after about a week and be ready for first harvest in five weeks. This crop can be snipped regularly for leafy morsels and will grow back again for several more cuts.

FEBRUARY TASKS

Parsnip time

Even before the last of the winter crop has been dug, it is time to start the new season's batch of this favourite root vegetable. Parsnips are long-growing in more ways than one, in the ground longer than any other crop and occupying their patch for over a year. In the days of my youth they were traditionally sown outdoors in February, the good old variety 'Tender and True' seeming able to germinate well and fight off the coldest conditions. My father always reckoned that a fall of snow covering them for a week or two after sowing sparked the dormant seeds into life.

Modern seeds seem reluctant to germinate, needing almost impossibly perfect conditions to get started, and I have tried many ways to get an even germination. Now I resort to 'trickery'. I sprinkle the seeds on a piece of kitchen towel and spray them with some tepid water, then I cover them with another piece of kitchen roll and spray this with the same water. Kept in a warm, even temperature with the paper moistened daily with a light spray of tepid water, the seeds start to put out tiny white roots after a week or so.

At this point I carefully pick up the germinating seeds with tweezers and transfer them to compost-filled toilet-roll tubes (or peat pots with their bottoms removed), three seeds per roll, and cover them lightly with compost. I stand the rolls in a tray in a warm place while the seeds complete their germination and send up their seed leaves, and then move them to a cold greenhouse to harden off before planting out. This method guarantees three seedlings per station when you eventually plant them out in the soil – no more sparse rows with large gaps and no forked roots from the disturbance of transplanting.

Chitting potatoes

'What do you mean by chitting?' I am often asked. Well, this is merely a means of encouraging the eyes on the potato tubers you have bought to grow a little before planting. Old egg trays are perfect for this, or you can use any other kind of tray that will support the tubers upright. Simply line up the seed potatoes in the trays with their eyes looking skyward, and keep in a frost-free place in partial light. Short stubby shoots will develop from the eyes by planting time, giving the tubers as much as six weeks' advance growth before they are consigned to the soil.

Out with those shallots

As soon as my shallots arrive and conditions are favourable they go out where they are to grow, the first plantings of the new season on the open plot. The bulbs are very hardy and soon start on their growth cycle up to a July harvest to supply those jars of pickled onions for my ploughman's feasts in the winter months. It's very satisfying, simply burying a bulb containing a complete embryo plant and then watching those first green shoots appear through the surface of the compost, knowing that new life truly is beginning. As a bonus I keep back six of the bulbs for planting in 6-inch (15 cm) pots in the greenhouse to provide early pickings of a spring onion 'substitute' to go with the first salad leaves and radishes.

Making beds

Once any frost has gone and the ground is dry enough after any rain, it is a good idea this month to start preparing as many as possible of the various beds you will need. The most important bed for me is the one where I will grow this year's onions.

To produce a good crop of these versatile vegetables means putting in a bit of time to produce a very fertile bed. The whole area gets a liberal

Preparing the onion bed

coating of well-rotted manure, which can be dug well in now, leaving the ground slightly 'lumpy' for the weather to break down into a finer tilth. There's still a few weeks for this as the onions will not go near the soil until the end of March at the earliest, and even then I only plant out onions as sets. The onions grown from seed for larger bulbs will not see Mother Earth until well into April, in the meantime remaining in the greenhouse, where they should grow big and strong in a more congenial environment.

First carrots

I start my earliest outdoor carrots indoors, rather like my parsnips, using bottomless peat pots in seed trays. I fill these with multi-purpose compost, sprinkle the surface of each pot with a few carrot seeds, and cover them with half an inch (13 mm) of sieved compost. 'Maestro' is my preferred variety as it has resistance to carrot root fly – this batch will eventually be planted outdoors without a fleece protection against the fly because sowing this early should avoid the first wave of the flying pest in an average year.

Carrots do not tolerate root disturbance, hence the bottomless peat pots. Once the pots are all sown, I lightly wet the surface with a spray of tepid water and then cover the whole tray with a sheet of glass to retain moisture and warmth. The seedlings should make an appearance in about three weeks. Starting with the carrots sown in my greenhouse container and border, I hope to have a plan in place for an unbroken succession of sowings right up to my maincrop later in the year. In this way I hope to harvest a supply that, with the help of the freezer, will last me the whole year round.

Once these seeds are sown, I turn my attention to the patch outdoors where these carrots will end up. The soil for them does not need manure but must be very friable and moisture-retentive. To ensure this I save a number of plastic bags filled with good leafmould, which is tipped on to the patch and dug well in to make a good growing area for these long-rooted plants. As I dig I fetch out as many stones as I can to prevent the roots from forking. All that remains is to repair some of the legs on the frames that will later cover the plants to protect them from their number one enemy, the carrot root fly.

Don't delay!

It might still be only February, but next month it all happens. March is always busy, made more so by fair-weather gardeners who will be waking up and packing the garden centres in their droves, so get down there now and make sure you are up to date with supplies.

For example, if you have not already done so go and buy your onion sets while they are still firm – next month they'll start growing – and spread them out in a seed tray in a cool place, ready for planting as soon as the weather and soil are right. Seed potatoes are on sale everywhere now, so it is a good moment to purchase all you need and get them chitted. Don't forget to spread your choice between early, second early and maincrop varieties, depending on when you want to harvest them: earlies in June, second earlies July to August, and maincrops late August to September.

Then, once you're all stocked up, get out those cloches and place them over the areas where parsnips, lettuces and cabbages are going to make their home according to your planting plans. This will allow the soil to warm up and get the young plants putting on growth sooner, without a shock from the cold ground.

Looking back

In the 1970s mushrooms became popular, and sites popped up in the valleys near the allotments to produce this trendy food. There were polytunnels everywhere filled with great bags of special compost on which the fungi were grown. Several times a year these tunnels were emptied out for restocking with fresh compost, and the discarded bags were brought along to the allotments and were given to the plot-holders for the cost of the diesel (just a few pounds in those days).

The spent mushroom compost was one of the best soil improvers and an extremely cheap way of 'bulking up' the soil. Then word got around at gardening shows, the compost became very sought after, and there was such a demand for it that gardeners went along to these mushroom farms to collect the compost themselves. The final irony in the history of this good, cheap compost was that very soon mushrooms imported from abroad became cheaper than any grown locally. The farms ceased to exist, and with them went our compost supply. Life seemed so · simple then.

FEBRUARY IN A NUTSHELL

Key jobs for FEBRUARY

- ✔ Purchase seed potatoes and set them up for chitting.
- ✔ Sow those parsnip seeds indoors.
- ✔ Plant shallots.

- ✔ Start some early potatoes in a drum in the greenhouse.
- ✔ Sow some early tomatoes.
- ✔ Sow carrots in the greenhouse for that early crop.

If you have time . . .

- ✔ Prepare your onion patch.

Looking ahead to MARCH

- ✔ Plant onion sets.
- ✔ Plant the first early potatoes on the plot.
- ✔ Harvest those forced rhubarb stalks.

- ✔ Sow tomato seed.
- ✔ Sow cucumber seed.

Checking newly transplanted seedlings

Thought for the month

I hope my almanac inspires some readers to give 'grow your own' a go. Start small – you do not need a full-size plot or large piece of garden to enjoy some fresh crops of your own.

Just a few pots standing on the kitchen windowsill can provide a tasty snack or two. Everyone at some time or other has purchased a plant or been given one as a present, and eventually this has passed on to the great compost heap in the sky, leaving its empty pot behind. All you need to do is pop along to your local garden centre and buy a small bag of seed compost.

While there, spend a few minutes browsing the racks and racks of seed packets and imagine yourself growing some of these for your own consumption. Don't get carried away: start with something simple that you like, and give it a try. Just follow the directions on the packet, and I am sure once you have tasted the fruits of your first attempt you won't be able to resist the urge to grow more.

From such simple, cautious beginnings every dedicated allotmenteer springs into being, and then the whole world is your garden. What are you waiting for?

MARCH

OH! WHAT A TIME OF GREAT EXPECTATION is the month of March. Stop, look and admire how nature has come through the long dark days and is bringing the start of a whole new season.

The clocks spring forward this month, heralding ever-lengthening evenings. No excuses now not to escape from the television and spend an hour or two out on the plot. As the the days get longer, you'll catch sight of little hints that bring optimism to the seasoned gardener.

Look carefully at the hedgerows, for example, and you will spot the hawthorn re-emerging after its winter slumber. The first measure of the beginning of spring on my plot is the tiny, unfurling leaves of my solitary gooseberry bush. When this comes to life I can start to ready myself for the first sowings of the season. So, life has begun again!

March is also the time when colour returns to the garden, albeit a predominance of yellow. The daffodils are reaching the perfection of their flowering season and move in unison in the March winds, while pale yellow blooms of primroses appear in the shelter of banks and trees. Garden centres respond by packing their benches with plants and there is a great urge to go out and buy, especially if March brings an early Easter, the traditional time when gardening starts in earnest.

Beware, though. If you have no means of protecting tender plants, keep your cash in your pocket for now and get out and enjoy your garden. There is plenty to do, and the earlier the ground is prepared the easier it will be to swing into action at the end of March, when the planting season really kicks off.

I am usually a happy chappie as the sowing and planting gains momentum in March – this is what gardening is all about for me and the hours just whizz by. Oh, happy days!

Early signs of revival

My gooseberry bush unfurling its leaves is one indication that spring is breaking. Another is that at last I will have some new fresh produce to grace my dinner table in the form of a few young rhubarb sticks, my first fresh dessert of the season. These I force each year under a plastic dustbin so that they are pale and tender. And the by-product of this first harvest is the leaves, which will give me protection for my brassica crops later in the season – the rhubarb leaves are cut off, stuffed in an old dustbin full of water, and allowed to brew into a smelly concoction for use later.

Fresh rhubarb is one reason I look forward eagerly to this month. Nature has been waiting too, as you can usually see all around you.

Harvesting
fresh rhubarb

Early one March I was working away at the bottom of my plot when I caught a silent movement out of the corner of my eye. Much to my surprise, floating on the warm air was a red admiral butterfly, its iridescent colours gleaming in the sunlight. Shortly afterwards it was joined by the rotund prop forward of the insect kingdom, a bumble bee wearing its club colours of amber and yellow stripes. These early emergent insects are desperately seeking a pollen source on which to feed. More signs of the changing seasons were evident in my blackberry bushes. Here a pair of blackbirds were seeking twigs and dry grass to furnish their new home. With the weather in their favour, they were busy building – no obvious credit crunch in the housing market in the bird kingdom, at least, as house construction raced ahead, and not just on my plot. All these creatures seem able to read the signs of nature's change far better than us.

Gardeners reawakening too

There are other strange stirrings down on the allotment, though. Just a few fine, sunny days and the fair-weather gardeners return. They are the ones who only use their plot in the best of the seasons and are never tempted to come there in rain, hail or snow. You can watch them as they stream through the gate with all their clean tools gleaming, and they are soon hard at it on the plot. Ground is tumbled over and weeds destroyed in the frenzy of activity everywhere.

I look at my plot during March and thank my lucky stars I've done so much winter preparation work. The manure has been put in the correct spots and dug in, the lime added where it is needed and most of the ground readied to host its new inhabitants. I check in the shed and there are my seed potatoes, their eyes bulging with strong, new shoots just raring to be set free. The onion sets too, loose in seed trays with their tanned skins rustling, are waiting to move out into their newly prepared bed.

Just another week and, if Mother Nature permits, there will be a mass exodus from that cosy shed to life in the wild.

Tales from the plot

It is that time of year once more when thrifty plot-holders have to dig deep into their pockets to pay for a whole year of pleasure. Yes, the annual rent for a plot is due this month, and everyone is grumbling. You would not believe that gardeners could be so steeped in the principle of never spending any money that paying the rent is a real wrench for many of them. Ours works out at the princely sum of four pence per day, and for what? Hours of pleasure, fitness and health, a wonderful social network and – if you play your cards right – a plentiful supply of fresh tasty crops all year round. The cost may be a bit higher in other parts of the country, but even so, in these days of rising costs, what else could you get for so little per day?

Talking of saving money, we noticed recently some tall structures rising up into the clouds on the mountainside above the plots. These, we are informed, will form a new wind farm. Now, the allotment fraternity are a very inventive group and, just as we run water hoses from the streams outside our fence, we are thinking that maybe we will be able to tap into this source of energy. There could be electric heaters in all the sheds and greenhouses, some really early tomatoes, and even floodlights to ensure twenty-four-hour gardening. Sadly, though, I reckon getting our hands on this tempting asset just beyond our plots might test the cunning of even the most resourceful of our allotmenteers. And normal gardening will resume once more.

'Nuts' and 'Bolts' have found a cheap alternative to bamboo canes for supporting their runner beans this year after discovering a willow copse that needed thinning. They duly arrived at the allotment with large bundles of straight willow poles over 9 feet (2.7 m) high. How they are going to pick the beans at the top of these tall poles, I don't know – it will certainly be a challenge – but it's a good use of cheap materials to be found all around.

While on the subject of bean poles, not a lot of people know that runner beans develop their flowers (and therefore their pods) at equal distances apart on the vine. So the thicker their supports, the more beans will be formed on a given height of plant, and really clever gardeners use very thick supports to achieve the heaviest crops. There you are, you learn something new every day in gardening.

Some gardeners make a lot of fuss about people buying vegetable plants as 'plugs' – young plantlets in tiny cells or modules. These may seem expensive compared with a packet of seeds, but there is nothing wrong if gardeners with limited space in which to grow vegetables buy plants as plugs and gain a head start over growing from seed.

This may offer a 'toe in the water' chance for anyone new to gardening to try out a few vegetables and experience the trials and tribulations of growing them, as well as taste the result of their first successes. Once they discover the vegetables they enjoy and how easy it is to bring them on from seedtime to harvest, they will no doubt move on to buying seeds and growing their crops from scratch.

How many of us have on occasions bought the odd plant or two of courgettes, peppers, pumpkins or tomatoes, all of them difficult to raise from seed if you don't have the luxury of a heated greenhouse to bring them on. Yes, they might cost more as plants, but if the balance sheet of growing your own took into account time spent raising crops, any economic argument goes out the window. How, for example, do you cost the true value of a hobby spent relaxing and enjoying yourself, with good health and wholesome food as by-products?

Many years ago growing fruit on the plot was an integral part of allotment culture, although the crops consisted mainly of redcurrants, blackcurrants and gooseberries. These provided the tasty sweets which always followed the main meal in valley households. For some reason this practice seemed to die off during the late 80s and 90s, with many of the old bushes being grubbed up.

But, as always, the pendulum swings back the other way, and there is now a growing trend towards fruit on allotments again. Not just the old traditional bush fruits but apples, pears, plums and cherries too. In fact, judging by the number of new trees that seem to arrive almost daily, there must be some special offers at local supermarkets! This has to be a good thing: with careful pruning and training, fruit trees take little space away from vegetables, and the potential savings from growing your own can be enormous.

Goosebery bush in leaf

Gardeners are inquisitive by nature. All the while they carry out their tasks they are observing others, and they are never too shy to call across, 'What are you doing there, then?' This is not always plain nosiness, but part of our grand tradition of learning and exchanging knowledge, and the way that the tricks of the trade have been passed on over the generations. Watch, observe and ask is a good creed for newcomers to adopt, while even the old hands can sometimes learn from the new kid on the block.

This is a great way for newcomers to find out from others' past experience what crops grow well on particular allotments, and to discover the local calendar for sowing and growing on a particular piece of land. There are many mysteries to solve out on the plot and no one knows all the answers. Gardening is a learning experience and transmitting knowledge through the annals of time is a great way to preserve the best skills. Old hands only pass on what has been passed on to them. This is a fine tradition, nowhere more evident than in the allotments community.

I was asked the other day why I transplant so many dozens of tomato seedlings, when I only need a few and give away the rest.

Well, there's the neighbour on one side of my plot who looks after the greenhouse in my absence, opening the door in summer and watering my plants. So I must look after him.

Then there is my neighbour on the other side, a retired builder who helps me out with all those DIY projects and saves me lots of cash. So he is high on my list.

There is another allotmenteer who owns a lorry, supplies my horse manure and helps improve my soil.

And the list goes on. Handing out a few tomato plants is a small price to pay for what I get in return. This is typical of life on the allotments, which is not about cash but about bartering and trading. No one goes away empty-handed.

Clive, one of our retired members, recently suffered a stroke but cannot stay away from the allotment site and the camaraderie of its people. With the better weather of early spring he is now a constant visitor, regularly joining us all in Albie's café for a drink and a chat. He looks better and feels happier every time he comes, walking more positively and enjoying the unique banter of plot-holders – you certainly would not come to the allotments for sympathy as that is in very short supply. The therapy seems to be working well. You cannot get that *kind* of recovery regime on the National Health Service!

All the woody material I had accumulated at the bottom of my plot was crisp and dry the other day, giving me the chance to try out the new metal bin I had converted into a brazier. A few pieces of newspaper, an armful of dry wood, and soon I had a good warm fire burning. Before long I was joined by Dai, who added his own supply of dry woody waste from his plot to my blaze. It was pleasant to stand there as the setting March sun added its dwindling warmth to that of the fire, making it difficult to leave that homely spot and do any more work on the cooling plot.

Bonfires inside are a different matter. One Sunday morning as I came into the allotments I was greeted by a large plume of smoke and the sound of harsh coughing. The thick smoke was pouring from a greenhouse just inside the gate, and there I found Julie (our only female plot-holder) wheezing and spluttering, trying to light her stove to make some coffee. She had used a great quantity of dry sticks and the greenhouse had quickly filled with smoke. No Fireman Sam needed, as we first feared: after opening all the windows and closing the damper, the smoke soon cleared and a hot fresh cup of coffee was my reward for the 'brave' rescue.

Last of a long crop

Early spring is a great time to start putting new plans into action. I have decided that my vegetable trug (see box on page 74) will be used to house some of my parsnips – the centre section of it is a good 18 inches (45 cm) deep, which is enough to house those long roots comfortably. So before I can get it ready to welcome its new guests, I have the pleasant (and also sad) job of harvesting the very last of my overwintered carrots.

With careful planning I have nearly nine months of fresh carrot harvests, and all is not lost over the remaining three because in my freezer there are already two large bags of this essential root crop, which should last me until the first sowings in the greenhouse are ready to harvest in April or May – so it looks as if it is possible to achieve a whole year of dining on my own carrots.

Vegetable trug, fully planted

Promising peas and beans

The first broad beans, sown in little polystyrene cups, are making good progress and are now poised to go out into the wide open spaces of the plot. The soil has been well manured ready to receive them and after being suitably hardened off they will be tough enough to overcome any cold snap that might yet occur. I harden them off in a cold frame with the top left off – there the cold March winds soon toughen them up.

The sweet peas, my colourful addition to the plot every year, have also been making good growth and by March should be about four leaves tall. Time for a little delicate surgery – find a pair of sharp nail scissors and 'off with their heads'. Well, it's not quite as savage as that, but the growing tips must be nipped out at this stage to encourage the plants to develop strong sideshoots and make bushy plants, rather than a single stem. More stems means the promise of more flowers.

Gradually the place is beginning to warm up and the landscape of the allotments is on the change, as are gardeners' faces. Happiness is radiating everywhere now the good days are back.

Broad beans

Tomato progress

When sown right at the beginning of March, tomatoes like my favourite 'Gardener's Delight' can produce a whole potful of healthy seedlings after just two weeks in the warmth of my airing cupboard. Even if a little tall, they can be transplanted deeply into 3-inch (8 cm) pots with the seed leaf level with the top of the compost – this will allow a good root structure to form and make well-rooted, sturdy plants, especially when grown in my mix of wormery and multi-purpose compost.

I sow complete packets, which can give me thirty or more early seedlings and perhaps twenty of 'Shirley' to grow on and fill my greenhouse in the summer, with plenty left over to share with my fellow allotmenteers. Between now and then they must be kept warm on the greenhouse staging until the first flowers appear, a signal to plant them out in my greenhouse border. It seems a long wait until late June before I can harvest firm red tomatoes for my salad bowl!

Companion plants

I'm always glad to see the broad beans make their exit to the cold frame, because space in the greenhouse is desperately needed this time of year for all the new sowings. Apart from the recently transplanted tomatoes, there are their greenhouse companions, the peppers and aubergines. Like the tomatoes they make very strong young seedlings in gentle warmth – my airing cupboard continues to pay dividends with these tender crops. I treat these in exactly the same way as the tomatoes, transplanting them into 3-inch (8 cm) pots when they make their first true leaf, again with their seed leaves almost touching the compost.

Companion planting

These tender crops are raised together: they must all get to know one another because they will be sharing the same accommodation all summer long. Tomatoes I have always grown, peppers came along later, and aubergines are my very latest experiment – my ambition has always been to harvest super, smooth mauve aubergines just like the ones you buy in the shops. They require some patience because they will not be ready to harvest for at least another twenty weeks, but the taste when they are home-grown and fresh is always worth waiting for.

Cabbage succession

I like a steady supply of summer cabbage throughout the season, and this is how I manage it. Early this month I take my packet of 'Primo' seeds plus a nine-cell seed-tray insert filled with good fresh, moist compost that is firmed into place. In each cell I sprinkle three seeds – they are large and easy to handle, so no trouble to sow in this fashion. Cover with a quarter of an inch (6 mm) of sieved compost and water lightly, then pop a cover over the tray and keep in a warm greenhouse, where seedlings should appear in seven to ten days.

Once they are well through, thin to leave one per cell, but don't waste the seedlings that you pull out: plant them in another cell tray and give them to your fellow gardeners, they are always welcome. Grow your tray on for about six weeks, when you should have strong plants ready to set out in the open ground after hardening off. If you repeat this every three weeks (there are plenty of seeds in a packet), you will ensure a season of juicy-hearted cabbage.

Papered carrots

For Christmas one year I received a paper-pot maker, which I use for sowing my early carrot seeds. I put the paper pots in small plastic pot 'outers' for support – they do not look pretty inside them but this method allows me to transplant the carrot seedlings without disturbing their roots (very important for any root crop). I start twenty pots of carrot seeds, with another twenty pots (without paper inserts) of beetroot sown two per pot. Sown in early March, both beet and carrots should be large enough to go out under a cloche in mid-April for my first salad root crops.

Making paper pots

MARCH TASKS

Preparing for potatoes . . .

By March the potato tubers that have been chitting in egg trays in my cool shed have developed strong green shoots and the first early varieties are ready for planting, so it's time to evict them from their comfortable home and plunge them instead into the darkness underground.

The potato patch has already had lashings of well-rotted horse manure thoroughly forked in. Now to get out the old mattock, dust off its winter cobwebs and plough a furrow in this rich, fine soil. A trench about 5 inches (13 cm) deep is ample, spread at the bottom with a scattering of blood, fish and bone to give the plants a good start in life – or in recent years pelleted chicken manure has become the new organic alternative, preferred by many.

Then space the tubers 10 inches (25 cm) apart along the trench, and simply drag all the soil excavated back over their heads. Don't forget to mark the rows, though, as there will be nothing to see for many weeks, and it will be late April before those large, broad leaves first push up through the soil.

. . . and next the onions

Those onion sets that have been languishing in the shed since February are next in line for release outdoors, after checking them over to remove any that might have gone soft. To me onions are one of the most precious crops on the allotment as they will feed me from August until about now when I am eating the last ones from store, so it is worth putting in a little extra time to prepare their new bed.

Weather permitting, I will have done a lot of the preparation during January and February: spreading manure and turning it in along with the green manure crop that has been growing since the autumn. I use a good amount of two-year-old manure, plus some old pigeon manure worked into the surface as an extra treat – old chicken manure is just as good with its high nitrogen content and lime to sweeten the soil. Just a word of warning, though, if you use these concentrated soil improvers: they must be aged for at least a year before use as otherwise they are too aggressive and can burn the roots.

Rake the soil to a fine tilth, then consolidate it by standing on a plank so that the onion sets have the really firm rooting conditions they love. Make a shallow drill just sufficiently deep to cover the little bulbs and draw the soil back over their tips, using your fingers to make sure they are below the surface and safe from the eyes of the preying birds. Some people net their onions to stop the birds pulling them up, but not me. I just do a deal with these feathered friends: you leave me alone and I won't bother you.

Carrot drums

You would think that with a 10-perch (250 m²) allotment I might have enough ground in which to grow all my veg. But there is something special about root crops sown in deep drums containing a mixture of horticultural sand and multi-purpose compost – the results would fare well in a flower and vegetable show!

This month I sow early 'Amsterdam Forcing' carrots in two big blue 45-gallon (200-litre) drums. These will be ready earlier than those out in the ground, and will be long and straight with no stones to make them fork or impede their growth. I sow the seeds in a spiral fashion, starting in the centre of the drum and circling outwards to the edge, keeping the spirals of the drill an even distance apart, roughly 2 inches (5 cm). Sow thinly and water well.

Sowing carrots in drums

To get them off to a good start in life I cover the top with fleece, which keeps them a little warmer while allowing moisture to percolate in and out. It also protects them from their arch enemy, the carrot fly. Don't be tempted to think that carrots sown some 4 feet (1.2 m) above ground will be completely immune: they may not suffer the same horrific attacks as unprotected soil-level carrots, but stray adult flies riding thermals can still reach this high, secret location.

High-status rhubarb

I was delighted to read that forced Yorkshire rhubarb has been given protected 'distinction of origin' status under EU law. This humble crop that people either love or loathe deserves a boost. The traditional tenant of a sunny corner on almost everyone's allotment, it figured large in my childhood while sweets were in short supply. My mum used to cut up a few stalks, pop them in a paper bag and sprinkle them with sugar, providing a healthy alternative to chocolate drops that made me many friends among my school mates. Thank heavens my father grew plenty of this wonderful crop!

Even though hardy and needing little attention, it cannot be ignored completely if you want a plentiful supply this month. A clean-up around its base in autumn, a good blanket of well-rotted manure plus a little feed in early spring, and your rewards will be great. If you have several crowns (their suitably regal name), then occasionally you can force a crop by covering one or two with a bucket or something similar to exclude the light.

This artificial environment fools the rhubarb into sending up those tender, pale pink early stalks that make an exquisite crumble, a true gastronomic delight. Don't carry out this forcing too often on the same crown, though, or you can severely weaken it. Every four to five years dig up the crown, remove the dead, woody portion and replant the youngest parts, each with a large bud. Then you will have another few years of high-status puddings.

Forcing rhubarb under a drum

Collars for cabbages

With summer cabbages growing vigorously under glass, now is a good time to prepare some collars to decorate the plants' stems at transplanting time.

There is nothing more disheartening than to set out any healthy member of the brassica family, only for the plant to turn red, then brown, and then collapse. These are the usual symptoms of an attack by the cabbage root fly, which lays its eggs at the base of brassica stems. These hatch out into tiny maggots that take up residence on the main root, feeding voraciously and quickly killing the plant.

Get some strong plastic material 5–6 inches (13–15 cm) wide (bricklayers' damp course is ideal for this) and trim it into squares. Use your scissors to make a cut from one edge to the centre, then branch left and right to make a Y-shaped flap to allow the collar to fit snugly around the stem of the plant. Arrange two in opposite directions, one above the other, to make an impenetrable shield against these burrowing pests, and you'll be well on your way to ensuring a plentiful supply of healthy greens.

Cabbage collar

Looking back (and forward)

For several months I was involved with another local allotment community that has been served with notice to quit by their landowner. These particular plots have been in existence for over a century, with many of the members having tilled that land for nigh on fifty years.

To lose part of their life in this insensitive and abrupt manner is like an amputation, which both brings a great deal of pain and causes the loss of something that has served faithfully over the years. Needless to say, members fought to reverse this decision within the law, showing every dogged determination to stay, but despite fighting the good fight were eventually beaten by the might of local government.

Too many allotments have been lost to the community under tarmac and concrete as land has risen in value in recent years. During the Second World War there were over 1.75 million plots in the UK as the 'Dig for Victory' campaign took effect. This fell to around a million plots during the mid-1950s. By the early 1990s land requirements for housing and a change in gardening culture meant that only about 400,000 plots were left in use. Times have changed now, however, and the twenty-first century is witnessing a huge revival in demand for a piece of ground on which to grow your own. Allotment sites up and down the country are full, with lengthening waiting lists.

To quote a famous speech, 'I have a dream' that by 2020 there will be over a million allotment plots in use once more. Food prices are increasing steadily, and there is a substantial move towards protecting the environment – no more flying food halfway across the world at huge ecological cost, for example, when it can be grown fresh in season on our own doorstep. And the most certain way to combat both of these unwelcome conditions is to go and get yourself an allotment!

My veg trug

This I have found is the perfect place to grow many crops away from marauding slugs and snails. It is a wooden box, 6 foot 6 inches (2 m) long by 3 feet (1 m) wide, with a deep centre for long root crops. It stands on six legs more than 3 feet (1 m) above the ground, so it escapes the attention of ground-feeding pests.

The trug is perfect for fast-growing salad crops, while at the edges trailing strawberries fare extremely well: they cascade down the sides, so the fruits are exposed to the sun as they ripen, with no splashes of soil to make them gritty. In fact it's a wonderful place to grow a multitude of crops, which can be tended without developing any backache, and this year the centre should make an ideal home for my parsnips, allowing the deep roots to grow free from canker.

Planting up the veg trug

Looking to next winter

It might only be the end of the third month of the year, but already it is time to sow some of those essential winter warmers – not out on the plot, I hasten to add, but in my cold greenhouse.

First there are my Brussels sprouts, at least two varieties such as early 'Brigitte' and late-maturing 'Wellington' to give me a full autumn and winter of firm buttons. I sow these in two separate half-size seed trays to allow plenty of surplus plants for fellow allotmenteers in exchange for other types of winter brassicas. They all need sowing now, because it is amazing how long they are in the ground before they return a harvest.

Also on the winter agenda is my other key crop for winter soups, my leeks. The varieties I use are 'Albana' and 'Musselburgh', again to provide a winter-long supply of these tasty vegetables. They are similarly sown in separate half trays for transplanting into larger trays at the seedling stage.

Spring feeding time

As well as starting to concoct my rhubarb-leaf brew to deflect cabbage white butterflies from my brassicas (see page 56), I like to get one of my feeding brews under way in March. As a child I was regularly sent to collect sheep manure from the hillsides around the allotments for my father's plot, an annual routine I continued for many years; but now in my old age I have it delivered from a local farm. This sheep manure is bagged up in a hessian sack, which is then suspended in a drum of water, covered with a lid and allowed to ferment for a couple of months or so. The result is a good liquid nitrogen feed for a range of plants. By making a start now the brew will be ready for when my feeding regime gets under way later in the season – it needs time to reach its best. One cupful in a 2-gallon (9-litre) watering can is a simple, effective and, above all, free way to ensure healthy plants. Just take a plastic bag with you next time you go for a walk in the country, and you could forget about buying fertilizer.

MARCH IN A NUTSHELL

Key jobs for MARCH

- ✔ Pinch out tips of sweet peas.
- ✔ Sow tomato seeds.
- ✔ Sow early carrots in greenhouse in bottomless pots.

- ✔ Sow cabbage seed in greenhouse.
- ✔ Plant early potato varieties.
- ✔ Plant out onion sets.

If you have time . . .

- ✔ Harvest forced rhubarb.

- ✔ Harden off broad beans.

Looking ahead to APRIL

- ✔ Take a few strawberry plants in pots into greenhouse for early crop.
- ✔ Cut twiggy sticks as pea supports.

- ✔ Sow lettuce seed in trays for early salad crops.
- ✔ Plant out onion seedlings.

Transplanting tomato seedlings

Thought for the month

Alarm bells have been ringing out the bad news that a survey indicates the gardeners' favourite ally, the hedgehog, is in rapid decline. Back in the 1950s, it seems, there were over 30 million of them roaming our country and munching countless slugs and snails as they went. Their population has now fallen dramatically to about 1.5 million.

Changes in farming methods and the spread of urban areas have made serious impacts on hedgehogs' freedom to roam. The generally milder winters of recent years, too, have affected them, causing them to appear from hibernation much earlier, before food has become plentiful.

Something that is very apparent to a gardener like me who has spanned this period is that slug and snail populations have rocketed, wreaking havoc for every organic gardener. As a young man with an allotment I never experienced so much destruction caused by slugs, I suspect because hedgehogs then had the upper hand and kept their numbers in control.

Imagine if our lost 28 million hedgehogs each ate just one slug per night, how many slugs might disappear from our gardens today! Is it too late, or can this valuable friend of ours be saved from extinction?

APRIL

APRIL CAN BE A DIFFICULT TIME for gardeners, because the weather may change at a stroke . . . and very often does. So we listen to the forecast every night, ready to rush back to the plot and protect those tender crops if a frost is mentioned. The very mention of that 'f' word sends shivers down my spine.

Nonetheless early April is a real vanguard of spring, and a time of great joy amongst allotment folk. At last those tiny seeds of many of our favourite vegetables can be sown, and there is an air almost of contentment on the plots as a new season begins in earnest. After long anticipation, it is time to get down to work.

This expectation is nowhere more obvious than in the warmer spots in our greenhouses. I find that by now mine in particular is bulging with seed trays, all housing the new season's crops. These have been transplanted from the crowded spot in the tray where they were sown to their individual compartments in yet another tray. There they can grow on during the next few weeks to make larger, more vigorous plants ready to face life on the open plot.

The evenings are not just noticeably drawing out more and more this month, but becoming warmer too, allowing us all to achieve more in the day and even return to the plot after tea. And as you work away in the late evening sunshine, what could be a more pleasurable accompaniment than the cheerful song of the birds in the adjoining hedgerow? Where else is it better to be than stirring the warmed soil with your hands, lured on by the expectation of what a few tiny seeds might become?

WHAT TO LOOK OUT FOR THIS MONTH

I am always hoping April showers will come my way and fall gently on the allotment – not too heavy, mind, nor too regularly, and interspersed with plenty of warm spring sunshine. Those would be perfect growing conditions to help all my early seed sowings on their way.

Already there is a little oasis of green appearing now the broad bean transplants have settled in well and are starting to bulk up. Other tell-tale signs of warmer days are the little flecks of green adorning fruit bushes as their tiny leaves start to unfurl.

But all is not happiness as the hungry gap looms. The last winter vegetables are being harvested – the remaining few leeks, for example – and soon there could be no fresh produce to fill our dinner plates. New crops are being sown, and some early cabbages and lettuces are well on their way under the cloches, but it will be a few weeks yet before these are ready. What shall we do? Shall we starve or (dare I say it) might we be seen down the vegetable aisles at our local supermarket? One has to eat!

First signs of trouble

We need to beware this month. The warmer weather that galvanizes gardeners into action also revives our enemies, and the early pests are about. Any tender new growth is the target of a feeding frenzy for marauding insects. First signs are in the greenhouse, where the chrysanthemums are tall and inviting, and there, suckling amongst this juicy growth, are a multiplying group of aphids. So it is off to the shed to dust off my pressure sprayer. Filled with tepid water and pumped up ready for action, its forceful spray soon eliminates these unwanted guests. I'll probably have to repeat this many times before I can gain control of the situation.

Knocking weevils off
broad beans

Back out on the plot my vigorous young broad beans already have tell-tale notches appearing on their leaves, a sign that the bean weevil has emerged from its winter slumber. These secretive pests are not so easy to control and a simple blast of water is not sufficient. It takes a lot of patience to knock them into a net and destroy them with the gardener's favourite weapon, the thumb and forefinger. This nibbling does not harm the plants too much once they start growing rapidly and it is only a minor inconvenience. But it is a sign that the annual war on pests is beginning again, a crucial part of the organic gardener's battle to win all those tasty crops.

Tales from the plot

In all my years on the allotments I have been relatively accident free, but my luck ran out one damp morning. Walking along the path to my shed I slipped on some wet manure, and after performing several desperate somersaults landed face down on the path.

Albie was standing in his greenhouse doorway, watching (and probably enjoying) my antics, and was quick to the rescue to help me up and clean off the dirt with lavish quantities of kitchen paper. Later I found myself in our local accident and emergency department, where I needed to have an injured knee and a number of ugly cuts patched up.

This left my wife to carry out the day's task of planting out my parsnips under cloches while I gave instructions from the sidelines. Fortunately I made a speedy recovery and normal service was soon resumed, but it just goes to show how easily and quickly accidents can happen even in the relatively safe surroundings of an allotment.

The coffee 'club' was in session as per usual one morning when Tony came across from his plot, clutching a pot housing an onion plant.

'What is that?' I asked.

'This is Ailsa Craig,' he replied.

'Well now you've named it, do you want me to christen it?' I said.

'You fool,' he replied. 'Does it look OK?'

It seemed fine to me, but I warned him not to plant it or the rest of its family out for a few more weeks yet as it was still a little early in the season. I should add that 'Ailsa Craig' is one of the best and oldest onion varieties, both for eating and for exhibition.

I don't know what it was about that week, but only a day or two later in came Paul carrying a large tray divided into numerous small compartments, in each of which he had growing a very healthy looking onion plant. He had planted his onion sets in compost in these trays to get an early start while the weather warmed up outside, and was concerned that the little bulbs at the bottom of the plants had gone soft and wrinkled.

This always happens and can look alarming until you are used to it. It makes sense when you remember that the bulb is the onion's cache of food to tide it over winter. When the plant starts growing again in spring and sends up its young green shoots, it draws the energy it needs from the food stored in the bulb, which seems to go down slowly like a balloon. In fact Paul's plants were fine and behaving normally. Another happy gardener!

Some plot-holders like to leave weeds as wildflowers or green manure, others hoe them off the moment their tiny leaves appear. It all depends on how you define a weed.

I remember one year being asked what ornamental plant would grow well on a panel of trellis someone had erected. I thought a clematis with its lovely foliage and gaudy large flowers would look good there, and he duly bought one. Lo and behold, it sulked and died.

Then I suggested a hardy honeysuckle, which would smother the trellis and, although not quite as showy as clematis, would provide fragrant blooms. Maybe he had less than green fingers, but this too failed to grow and soon gave up the ghost.

Some weeks later I asked him about his trellis and he proudly invited me over to see his new arrival. The whole panel and its wooden supports were smothered in a rampant mass of green leaves interspersed with large, pure white blooms. Unknown to him convolvulus or bindweed roots had found their way to the bottom of the trellis, and he was feeding and nurturing this lovely weed, which rewarded him with this stunning display of healthy foliage and gorgeous blooms.

Truly, one man's weed is another's pride and joy!

Do you ever forget what you were doing when you're interrupted in the middle of a task? There I was, steadily planting my second early potatoes. I had just opened the trench and dug in some well-rotted manure when I was called for coffee in the shed on a neighbouring plot.

After the obligatory break (social life is important on the allotments) I returned to the task in hand. I promptly started to back-fill the trench with all the soil I had dug out when my neighbour said, 'Wouldn't it be a good idea to put some potatoes in that trench first before you fill it in?'

I would have been looking in vain in a few weeks' time, scratching my head and wondering why nothing was coming up in this row. It only goes to show that ageing brain cells are easily distracted and do not respond like they used to.

There is a greater awareness these days of the need to protect crops during the early part of the year, especially here in the Welsh valleys, and so cloches have become a dominant landscape feature on our hillside in recent years. Not that many of us have the cash to spare for some of the more elaborate structures from local garden centres. Just a few lengths of wire or tube bent to make the supporting structure for a piece of recycled polythene and behold, a cloche is born.

I prefer to use horticultural fleece as the covering over home-made plastic hoops. Fleece involves only a very modest outlay of cash, and has the benefit over polythene of 'breathing'. Its microporous holes allow moisture to pass through, keeping the soil damp, and when the sun shines any excess moisture can evaporate back out. This prevents the soil from drying out too much, but avoids the steamy hot atmosphere under plastic that encourages fungal diseases.

Whatever you use, though, it will help create a snug home this time of year for all those early sowings, and give them a quicker start in life.

In my early years on the allotment there were very few buildings taking up space on the 10-perch (250 m²) plots – you needed all of your

Home-made cloche

ground to supply enough food to supplement the household budget.

Nowadays hardly a plot exists without its own custom-built shed and greenhouse. The shed is a must for storing all those bits and pieces that gardeners collect: trays, old buckets, lengths of wood, plastic sheeting and many other throwaways find a home here. Maybe they never see the light of day again, but to the discerning eye other people's discards have a future use, albeit as yet unknown.

As for the greenhouses, many of those built on our site have risen like a phoenix from the ashes: countless old double-glazing units have been salvaged from skips to craft into a suitable home for our precious plants. My own greenhouse started life as a 'prefab', one of those temporary houses erected during the war years. Without these structures it would be difficult to raise early plants and steal a march on nature, and there would certainly not be such an abundance of crops like tomatoes and cucumbers during the summer on this wet Welsh hillside.

There must be something inbred in a gardener's make-up that hates all waste and can find a way to reuse other people's 'rubbish'. Composting discarded foodstuffs to make that wonderful material for adding back to the soil is commonplace these days. Recycling goes much further than that on an allotment, though, and most waste materials play some kind of role in the gardener's eternal grand design.

For some time now I have been singing the praises of a wormery. About the same time as wormeries first arrived in my gardening repertoire, I acquired two Bokashi units, airtight bins in which all food material can be composted with the addition of a bran full of micro-organisms. The material breaks down to a concentrated liquid which can be tapped to feed crops, while the remaining waste can be added to the compost heap after six weeks to accelerate decomposition.

Wormery providing liquid feed

Compost produced inside wormery

I saw the real benefits the first summer when I used the liquid for feeding my hanging baskets and pots, which were the best ever. But little did I know that the units would also significantly impact on my seed sowing and bringing on the resultant seedlings.

One of the problems encountered when raising plants from seed is that damping off often occurs in the seed trays while seedlings are still small, and once it starts this fungal disease can spread quickly, killing off whole trays at a time. So I added a small drop of the liquid drained from a Bokashi unit to the water I use to spray the seedlings once they have germinated. This completely eliminated any losses from damping off, even seeming to bring a sparkle into their young lives, and they grew strong and healthy with the benefit of this 'elixir'.

This is another example of the way that going organic has brought new methods and unexpected rewards into my long gardening career. Never again will I resist the bold step of embracing new-fangled ideas with open arms to see if they work. Some of them fail, of course, and these can then be consigned to the scrap heap (not the compost heap!), but others will bring unexpected success. It's the same with trying new varieties of vegetables – never dismiss anything before you try it.

PLOT PROGRESS

'Wild gardening' seems to be fashionable these days on allotments, with all sorts of plants muddled up together. Now, much as I admire wildflowers and wildlife generally, I don't think random planting has a place on the vegetable plot. Mine is very symmetrical, dominated by straight lines, because I have found that crops are more easily cared for if they are regimented, with weeds immediately distinguished from vegetables by their disorderly appearance. All it takes is an April shower and the weeds appear as a definite green hue on the barren soil between rows, galvanizing me to reach for the hoe and also to raid my seed tin and transform the plot with more straight lines.

Those elusive caulis

Cauliflowers are what I call my nemesis. One of the best vegetables you can have, they are also one of the hardest to grow, and I have tried very often, using different methods and varieties, all without success.

But never say die. I have decided to put them back on my sowing agenda, this time trying seeds of the variety 'Crispus', which is resistant to club root. With an early start they were growing on well by April, and I prepared a really rich piece of ground and panned it down very hard. These are supposed to be the perfect conditions for growing caulis, a greedy crop that needs firm ground to produce those large tight white curds. All I need after that is to organize plenty of water – another essential – and I'm beginning to dream of a dozen perfect specimens growing on my plot.

Watch out for Jack Frost

The plot is usually filling up nicely with a succession of crops as the month progresses, but sometimes things can be going too well. I get worried when my early potatoes thrust their large green leaves through the surface of the soil, for Jack Frost still roams at night during April in this part of the world. So as soon as any potatoes pop their heads above the ground, it is out with my special wide-bladed hoe to draw earth up and over the emerging shoots. This helps keep them safe for a night or two, but I need to keep an eye on them after that. It only takes a little sunshine and warmth, and they quickly pop through again.

Potatoes popping through

IN THE GREENHOUSE

Last but not least

Before I gratefully hand the airing cupboard back to my wife for her sole use, I have one last sowing to make and keep in there. With the tomatoes, peppers and sweetcorn doing well in the greenhouse, it is time to sow my cucumbers.

This crop is not remotely tolerant of cold. It needs a consistently warm temperature to germinate well, at least 21°C (70°F) with an uninterrupted growth cycle, so I start them in the cupboard among the clean shirts and sheets.

As soon as their large leaves poke through the compost the seedlings come straight out on to my warm windowsill, and I can finally relinquish the airing cupboard for another year. After a few more weeks' growth, the cucumbers will be ready to transplant into the corners of my greenhouse. I can hardly wait!

Little and often

Sometime this month the early carrots and beetroot sown in pots should be ready to be freed from the greenhouse. If conditions are in their favour outside, I just need to fork the ground over lightly and rake in some blood, fish and bone, and they can be carefully planted out.

The season is still young, however, and although the plants have been thoroughly hardened off I do not want to expose them to our Welsh weather just yet. A plastic cloche can give them some essential protection while boosting their growth to give an even earlier crop – this kind of precaution is a vital part of the quest to provide a long and steady supply of vegetables year-round.

Then, with those precious little pots freed up, I immediately sow some more beetroot seeds in them, and keep these in the greenhouse to begin the cycle all over again. At the same time I fill a few of my buckets with compost and sow the next generation of radishes and spring onions to keep in the greenhouse until they are large plants, when the buckets can be moved outside the door.

It is this little-and-often policy that ensures my continual summer sequence of harvests.

Moving with the times

For a few weeks now the greenhouse shelves have been groaning under the weight of plants sitting there waiting to move on to the outside cold frames for hardening off, before they are planted in the open ground to grow on to maturity.

No sooner are enough of these plants on the move outdoors than the staging is gradually removed. This allows me to prepare the parts of the greenhouse borders previously covered by staging with new soil, plenty of well-rotted manure and compost to make a home for this year's crop of tomatoes, cucumbers and peppers. Oh, those glorious days of feasting are not far away now!

Bonus berries

While cleaning up the strawberry bed one year I happened to find half a dozen strong runners that I had managed to miss earlier. I carefully forked them up, potted each one in a 6-inch (15 cm) pot, and tucked them under the greenhouse staging. After several snug weeks there they made great progress and developed into decent-size plants, large enough to remove from hiding during April and transfer to a sunny position near the glass. With a feed of liquid seaweed extract every time I watered I had them flowering, fruiting and in the dish with a helping of fresh double cream well before Wimbledon. Very often in gardening a calculated gamble turns up trumps.

Sweetcorn to die for

Three summers running resulted in disappointment with my sweetcorn. It is a crop that likes a fairly long growing season and lashings of hot sunshine, so a Welsh allotment is right at the edge of its comfort zone. I can't express my dismay when the crop fails, for those large juicy cobs full of sweetness and flavour are one of late summer's great joys.

So every year I try again, refusing to surrender in my annual quest. April is the month when I sow the large yellow seeds (with a wish and a prayer) in my warm greenhouse in root trainers to avoid any root disturbance when planting them out. They should make stout young plants ready to go out on the plot in mid-May. With the seeds safely started, all I can do is dream of cutting a fresh cob and cooking it at its peak of perfection, ideally within two hours of harvest.

Planting sweetcorn

Looking back

Many years ago, when I first took on an allotment plot at the age of eleven, our site on the side of the mountain was laid out with three tiers of plots, forty-two of them in all and every one in full cultivation.

During the 1980s, though, demand for allotments was at an all-time low and plots began to fall out of use. The highest of them up the mountainside were the first to become vacant, and with no further demand for them they were soon reclaimed by nature. As if from nowhere appeared lots of young saplings, which have grown into a miniature forest over the last twenty years.

Wayne and his mate finally decided these trees were shielding too much light from their plots and began the task of reclaiming some of this lost land. Since then there has been a constant buzz of a chainsaw and an ever-increasing pile of logs building up. It is surprising how much extra light has already reached the adjoining plots since this work commenced, making you realize just how surely and stealthily nature reclaims what is neglected by man.

Now there is a growing demand for allotments once more, we are hoping some intrepid allotmenteers might see this ground being reclaimed and want to take on one of these plots again. It would bring back many happy memories for me if all these plots were back under cultivation, just as they were in the late 50s and early 60s. With the constantly rising cost of food it would be great to see all the plots back in use and filled to capacity.

April is a lovely but capricious month – it can bring a warm sunny foretaste of summer or ooze past as winter has its last fling – and it is often hard to know what to do and when. My rule is to get all those seed packets of my favourite vegetables lined up and, to some extent, ignore the sowing times on the packet. These are only rough guides based on average years, but they take no account of locality or conditions on the ground, and it is Mother Nature who always has the final say about when to plant them. I like to test the ground with the palm of my hand, and if it feels warm and moist then get the seeds in because these are the perfect conditions for germination.

Sow first outdoor carrots . . .

Having sown my earliest carrots in drums it is now time to take action on the main sowing outdoors as soon as conditions are right – three rows of them, 20 feet (6 m) long and 6 inches (15 cm) apart.

Irregular germination of these tiny seeds seems to be a common problem these days, so I give them some special treatment. After drawing out my drills in the soil with a hoe, I line each furrow with seed compost. The seeds are sown in this and covered over with a little more compost as well. I find this mimics being sown in a seed tray, in near perfect conditions that greatly enhance the germination rate.

The compost holds enough moisture round the seeds while they germinate, and being darker than the surrounding soil it warms up quickly in the spring sunshine, providing exactly the two main conditions seeds need to grow.

. . . and then protect them

As soon as the carrots have been sown, they need protection from their number one enemy, the carrot root fly. During the cold winter months I knock up some wooden structures to fit over the carrot rows, and these act as supports for the Enviromesh netting that I drape over them and fix securely against these mischievous predators.

In the past I have shielded carrots with horticultural fleece on supports, but this has been less effective during the wet summers we have had recently. With my new method the plants are completely enclosed, so the flies will have to come equipped with wire cutters if they wish to feed on my plants this year. The carrots are not at risk yet, but the mesh also keeps out a degree or two of cold, so fixing my frame and cover immediately after sowing creates a warmer spot in which they should grow faster.

Transplanting onions

Before retiring to the comfort of my greenhouse again, there is usually one more job to perform out in the open air. My young onion plants, started from seed way back in early January, should be ready by now to fill the remaining space in my onion bed. They have had two weeks' hardening off in the cold frame, and ought to be toughened up enough to go out and face conditions on the plot.

Planting out onion seedlings

I grow several varieties (mainly 'Mammoth', 'Red Mammoth' and the exhibitor's standby 'Kelsae'), more as a bit of fun to try to achieve those super-size bulbs you see on the show bench. They are an enjoyable gamble, but I never grow them in place of onions from sets, which are the mainstay of my winter store – onions grown from seed need using up first as they do not store well.

Lettuce lesson

For many years I sowed lettuce in long rows across the plot and then spent an age thinning them out. After several weeks more I would always have a glut of lettuces, plus enough surplus to feed the neighbourhood. Then it was a case of famine for several weeks while I sowed the next row . . . and the same scenario would play itself out again.

I have finally learned a sound lesson from that and now sow my lettuce in cell trays with six compartments, one tray of an iceberg lettuce variety and another of the red, leafy 'Lollo Rosso'. When the first trays of seedlings are emerging, I sow the next pair in the same way. Then when the first lettuces are planted out the empty trays are filled with a new sowing yet again. By repeating this pattern I have a steady sequence of mature lettuce from late May right through to the first frosts. There are still a few to spare and share, but above all an unbroken supply of fresh lettuce for myself and no wasted space on the plot.

The pumpkin challenge

Every year I try to grow a larger giant pumpkin than before, but these wandering plants do take up a lot of my precious ground. Then one year a colleague on the allotment was not using his entire plot, so I saw my chance and undertook to dig the rest and keep it clean so that I could grow this roving monster there. With the deal agreed and half the plot prepared, I dug out a large hole and filled it with well-rotted manure to sustain the beast.

Planting out pumpkin

Each plant can fill a patch 10 feet (3 m) wide, with each stem roaming over 24 feet (7 m) just to produce one massive pumpkin. It's hard to appreciate how much can come from a single small seed. I sow three this month, choosing the strongest to go on and occupy the prepared site. This solitary plant will be treated well, even spoiled, to produce (if all goes to plan) a pumpkin 160 lb (70 kg) or more, which is weighed at the end of the season and auctioned each year for a good cause.

Break for 'housework'

During a lull in all the seasonal tasks on the plot, I set off to attack the hedge at the lower end of the allotments for an hour or two. The trees growing there are reviving from their winter sleep, and before the sap starts rising too much I take my loppers and collect a large bundle of prunings to add to the pile of privet I collected last autumn – these twiggy sticks make great supports for my peas. This routine trimming and tidying also helps to improve the amount of light getting through at the bottom of the plot. Most vegetables like a sunny, open site, but I am amazed by how much these trees grow every year and if left to their own devices will soon completely shade the bottom of my plot. So that's two jobs accomplished in one: less shade on the plot and several bundles of free pea sticks.

Weedy warning

With increasing warmth and day length, it is not just the seeds which I have painstakingly sown that start making an appearance on my plot. There is also a suspicious mist of green from the pesky annual weeds that soon make their presence felt once spring arrives. Wherever do they all come from?

This is the signal to take instant action before they make much progress in their battle to outgrow and outwit my precious crops. I wait for the sun to rise high in the sky, and then, with a few swift strokes of my razor-sharp hoe, root and leaves are quickly separated. Lack of roots and a dose of hot sun quickly put paid to these intruders. But take heed: they or their friends will return, so keep that hoe sharpened and at the ready.

One tip I always pass on to new tenants on our plots is to not forge ahead with digging and planting without looking behind occasionally. As you progress, those cunning weeds soon move into the newly tilled ground and sown vegetable rows. Stop, look back, and clear them out before marching ever onwards.

Blight-free potatoes

One more job for April while the going is good, and that is to plant the last of my potatoes, the maincrop to lift for storing over winter. The wet mild summers we seem to get these days are perfect for encouraging the spread of potato blight, and after less than perfect results with other maincrop kinds I have reverted to the Sárpo family of varieties.

These Hungarian-bred potatoes have been developed to tolerate or resist blight more than others, and as they are trialled in Wales ought to be good for my plot. I have had great success before with 'Sárpo Mira', a good cropper that also seems to be drought-resistant and unattractive to slugs – what more could anyone want? They may not be as tasty as many other potatoes, but it looks as though I need blight protection to guarantee some disease-free spuds for the winter.

Planting maincrop potatoes

APRIL IN A NUTSHELL

Key jobs for APRIL

- ✔ Plant out lettuces and cabbages under cloches.
- ✔ Attack early aphids in the greenhouse.
- ✔ Watch out for the first attack of bean weevils on broad beans.
- ✔ Earth up early potatoes to protect them from frost.
- ✔ Sow cucumber seeds in pots in a warm place.

If you have time . . .

- ✔ Keep early weed seedlings at bay by regular hoeing.

Looking ahead to MAY

- ✔ Erect runner bean canes ready for early sowings.
- ✔ Continue to earth up potatoes.
- ✔ Plant out Brussels sprouts.
- ✔ Plant out tomatoes in the greenhouse.
- ✔ Plant some marigolds in the greenhouse to ward off aphids.

Blasting blackfly

Thought for the month

The growth in demand for allotments by people with little or no garden of their own and who want to grow crops has meant waiting lists everywhere and a shortage of suitable land where these aspirations can be achieved. Hence the initiative for 'land share' groups, which are springing up all round the country as demand continues to exceed supply.

People who have land – part of a field, a whole back garden or just a spare bed or two – but lack the ability or desire to cultivate it share with keen gardeners who want space to grow their own. This is obviously beneficial to both parties, especially if any arrangement includes sharing the produce. We all have to pay rent for our plots!

I applaud this idea provided it is sensitively managed so that all parties are satisfied. It is one way to overcome the problem of land shortage, but should not distract attention from the obligation of local authorities to provide ground for allotments wherever there is a demand, rather than try to close them and sell the land, as seems to be happening all too often.

MAY

WHAT A LOVELY MONTH MAY IS! The days continue to lengthen, while the evenings can be warm enough to sit outside and admire the changing scenery. The maple trees at the bottom of my allotment are now in full leaf, with brilliant red hues that make a fantastic backdrop to my plot as it turns ever greener.

As I look into the distance beyond the various plots this month, the valley will be returning to its summer splendour, all the fields and large expanses of deciduous forest turning the landscape into a kaleidoscope of many shades of green. Is it any wonder I have to drag myself away from the allotment as the sun sets and night's shadows fall? That ten minutes admiring the view after a hard day's work makes the perfect end to a pleasant day.

May is also a month I welcome because it heralds the end of the 'hunger gap', the season when the last winter produce has been harvested and the first crops of the year are not quite ready to pick. It seems a sorry affair when you grow your own if you then have to rely on another supplier to put food on the table. But as the month progresses the plot will rapidly fill up: there shouldn't be long to wait before I can look forward to the first real harvests as my reward.

Already rhubarb will be cropping well and providing plenty of sweet dishes. Lettuces growing under a cloche should be ready to cut now and the cabbages sharing the cloche with them only a week or so away from my dinner plate. I'll soon be back in control of my own dietary needs, able to feed my family again.

Busy! Busy! That is the feeling I always get in early May. Throughout the month there's a steady procession of seed trays from greenhouse to cold frame, from cold frame to soil, and the plot rapidly begins to fill with the results of all the seed sowing and transplanting.

There is also the feel-good factor as tiny green seed leaves emerge from the plain dark soil, heralding the appearance of parsnips and carrots sown only a few brief weeks ago – new life when the month is sometimes barely a week old! This is a good indication that the soil is warming up, with conditions favouring this burgeoning – otherwise plants would still keep their heads below ground. They are too experienced to take chances.

This is the time of year when I arrive at the plot and take time to walk around, observing what is happening rather than rushing into some preplanned activity. Very often there will be a tiny green haze forming among the treasured vegetables, a sign that weeds are also springing into life.

Wherever do these intruders come from? Every year I endeavour to keep them under control, but each spring someone else's weeds manage to take up residence on my plot. They need attacking while still small, before they can take hold and smother the precious vegetables, and the hoe is the answer. On a sunny day hoe among the crops, leaving the chopped-off weeds to wither in the sunshine. In wet weather, however, hand-weeding is the best solution because otherwise the cut weeds just stand up again and continue growing.

That first harvest of new potatoes

Elsewhere on the plot larger eruptions of soil show where early potatoes are making their entrance, always a welcome sight as long as it's not unseasonally cold. Before I head for home, though, I have one more exciting task to perform. My extra-early potatoes planted way back in February in a drum in the greenhouse look as if they might be ready to yield a crop. I roll up my sleeves and plunge my hand into the drum, and there I find some white, egg-sized new potatoes to grace my dinner plate. These underground treasures are a joy to behold and are another crop to add to the growing May harvest.

Early potatoes

Tales from the plot

All is not peaceful on the allotments.

There is a steady hum of cultivator motors this month as the soil is turned for more planting. Dave J and Bob are busy toiling away and the ground looks really good in its finely tilled state. Still, once the job is done peace and tranquillity will resume on our quiet hillside.

There's a new addition to the growing range of businesses springing up in the sheds and greenhouses on the site. We now have Bob's Bar.

During a recent minor heatwave demand for Albie's coffee diminished as we all went in search of something more refreshing. So enterprising Bob got hold of a few cans of cider, immersed them in his water barrel to keep them cool – and lo, 'Bob's your uncle', a cool drink was on offer to wet those dry mouths and bring renewed vigour to our gardening activities. The enterprise of these innovative allotmenteers!

A cry for help rang from the middle of the allotment site this week. Gary's broad beans were dying.

'What's up with these then?' he asked sorrowfully.

'You haven't used fresh manure on this ground before planting?' I wondered.

With bowed head he replied, 'Yes.'

And there you have it in a nutshell. 'You're killing them with kindness,' I said.

So beware: never use manure while it's still fresh. It must be at least six months old and well weathered.

The 'Ground Force' gardening team were called to the rescue the other week, after Albie had to go into hospital for a minor operation. This knocked him up for a bit and threatened his pride and joy: his runner beans that were desperate to be planted out.

So the team swung into action. Bob brought his cultivator and turned the ground over to a fine tilth. Next to come was Jeff, who put up all the sticks, and I contributed my bit by tying them in my unique way.

Two days later Albie was able to plant his beans at the base of the row of sticks and was a happy man once more, now he was back on track. Protected with some large plastic sheets against any chilly nights, the vines were soon twining their way skywards. Remember, Albie, there are three candidates here to help you use up those early bean pickings!

Last year I tried controlling slugs the safe way with nematodes. This is a favourite organic method using no pellets or chemicals. You simply water the ground with the compound the nematodes arrive in. These useful parasites then seek out the pests and feed on them, hopefully wiping out the whole population. The trouble is, new reinforcements from further up the hillside keep on coming in to replace their deceased comrades.

So I decided to try a new weapon in my armoury, developed by Cardiff University and based on that Biblical gift of myrrh. When mixed with sawdust it forms a repellent barrier that actually becomes more active when wet – unlike more conventional barriers such as eggshells and coffee grounds, which lose their effectiveness as soon as they get wet, allowing all the slugs and snails to calmly glide over them to get at your precious plants.

Although this new slug control worked for me and took at least two months to lose its effectiveness, the university could find no one interested in developing it as a commercial product, and sadly it disappeared from the radar. It was, admittedly, expensive and market research felt it would not be a winner.

Occasionally I wonder why we take on gardening when sometimes it can seem like a perpetual battle. But the answer is very simple: it's because the hobby is fun and the rewards so great that it is always worth the effort.

Walking around the allotments last week I almost leapt out of my skin. As I was passing Gary's plot I was startled to see a tall, grotesque figure out of the corner of my eye. It stood there, quite motionless. I quickly realized that it was not human, but a scarecrow that Gary had erected to keep the wood pigeons off his freshly planted cabbages.

Oh, the joys of getting older . . . and more forgetful. I am forever putting down tools and losing them or forgetting to put them away.

Then the other week I sowed some radish seed in what I thought was an empty bucket in my greenhouse. The little seedlings were just emerging from the soil when they were shouldered aside by some big potato shoots erupting from below, in the same bucket. Some weeks ago I had a couple of second early tubers left over and decided they might as well go in this empty bucket, but as I didn't add a label I completely forgot about them.

Things turned out well, as it happened, and my lapse of memory gave me two crops for the price of one. The radishes flourished and were consumed in a very short time, then the potatoes grew on to supply a second crop from the barrel – much like using radishes as a row marker for slower-growing seeds.

I dread to think what I might double-sow out on the plot itself, though!

The seasons are ever changing and this year has been no different. March saw an early spring, for example, and the urge to rush ahead was difficult to curb, but curb it I did. The reward was a wet and cold April, which meant the sowing and planting routine was curtailed by Mother Nature. There is no such thing as a sowing calendar that allows for these climatic changes, and it is best to garden by 'feel' and experience. You can usually catch up in May.

But shock, horror! When I peeped out of my curtains first thing the other morning, there on the lawn was a carpet of brilliant white frost –

charming in February, perhaps, while everything is dormant, but not a welcome sight in mid-May.

I hurried up, ate a quick breakfast and rushed off to the plot to see what damage this unexpected chill had wreaked. As I feared, my early potatoes sported blackened tops, despite my earthing them up two days previously after the forecasters warned of cold nights. But this was to no avail as the impatient spuds were on the move and determined to push back through the surface. So they paid the price, which was a check to growth and a delay in their quest to produce an early harvest. There's nothing you can do then but hope they'll send up new shoots soon after all chances of frost have passed.

I walked round a little dismayed by this unexpected frost damage and was interested to see the possible effects elsewhere on the allotments. Many plot-holders had suffered the same fate, although one or two had escaped damage by draping fleece over their crop. I was amazed by Jeff's and Tony's runner beans, however, as these appeared to have survived intact and free from damage simply by being surrounded with plastic sheeting. That was enough to keep Jack Frost from a tender tropical vegetable.

We were sitting on the bench during one of those brief spells of May sunshine we sometimes get, when Albie said to Brian, 'One of your tomato plants doesn't look too well.'

So off Brian went to check on it, and I was summoned too for a second opinion on its health. When I walked into his greenhouse, there in the corner was a tomato plant with its lower leaves looking distinctly yellow. I bent down, grasped its stem and looked intently at my watch.

'What are you doing?' Brian asked.

'Taking its pulse,' I replied, 'and that seems fine to me.'

'You fool!' he retorted.

I was right, though, and the happy outcome was that the tomato was fine and recovered well once its old lower leaves were removed.

It's amazing how the allotments have been transformed since we had the new road through them. All along the edges of the road little pockets of flower beds are beginning to appear. This started with Dave H soon after the road was built, then Dai and Gary joined in this exercise in 'flower power', creating welcome areas of colour and beauty at the roadside. What a difference this has made to the look of the place – we're certainly moving upmarket these days. Long may it continue!

Terry S seems to be making a contribution, too. On his plot below mine the other day I noticed an unfamiliar rustling in the breeze, and there, whirling round at great speed, was a tall yellow and orange windmill. I thought Terry might be generating his own power to heat and light his greenhouse – it's the fashion, after all. But no, it was simply his colourful attempt to repel pigeons from his new cabbage plants.

I find it mildly amusing when I read all the articles in the press about the need to recycle and conserve water. They stress these measures are essential if we are to 'save' the planet.

When I look back to my early days of gardening in the 1950s recycling was commonplace, not to save the planet but because all allotment holders were thrifty by nature. Other people's waste was widely used on the plots, for example, to build sheds and greenhouses. Water was always stored in barrels filled by rain cascading off these old sheds and greenhouses during the wet winter season – again, not with the conservation of water as the main objective, but simply because it made the job of watering the plot a lot easier if the water supply was close to the point of use.

I am lucky on my plot. The allotments are surrounded by high hillsides criss-crossed by fresh mountain streams full of clear, pure water that runs freely and every day replenishes my water butt supply solely by gravity. It gets used up steadily: until my young plants send their roots deep into the damp subsoil they need regular wettings, and I swear my right arm is three inches longer than my left, thanks to the constant back and forth with heavy cans.

PLOT PROGRESS

All over the plot rows of young vegetables should now be quite distinct. This is a good time to get out that hoe and keep those weed seedlings from getting a foothold, at the same time keeping the soil loose and free so that any May showers can penetrate and save watering later. Hoeing is a job I like to do on most of my visits and it helps the plants speed ahead.

Although my soil is normally in good heart from all the natural supplements I've dug in, I like to top up this fertility about now. Crops that have been in the ground for a while may have suffered severe chilling from the wind we get down our valley, sometimes turning garlic and broad beans a bit yellow. With the weather warming up it's time to treat these to a feed of fertilizer to bring colour back into their leaves.

The type of fertilizer you use will depend on whether or not you favour organic methods. If you use chemical fertilizers a mix of superphosphate and a handful of sulphate of ammonia will do the trick. I like to spread a 50:50 mixture of dried concentrated manure and blood, fish and bone among the onions, shallots, garlic and broad beans. I do this when there are showers about so that it's quickly absorbed into the soil, especially when hoed in, and gives plants a welcome boost.

Rhubarb alchemy

I'll have been harvesting rhubarb for some weeks by now – the enjoyment of rhubarb crumble never seems to cease. The huge leaves from these tasty stalks go into a plastic dustbin full of water, where they are stirred every few days until they smell like an evil broth.

There are usually a few sightings of cabbage white butterflies fluttering round the plots in May, and my cabbages are big enough to support a whole family of their young, those voracious green caterpillars that munch the leaves into bare netting. I soak the cabbages with the smelly rhubarb broth to ward off the little butterflies and force them to go elsewhere to lay their eggs. The smell soon fades to *our* noses, but happily lingers much longer on the proboscis of a butterfly.

Topping beans

The broad beans, which seem to have been planted so long ago, have finally reached full height this month, and the beans are starting to swell. This is a good time to take out the plants' green growing tips before those hungry blackfly take up residence in their favourite spot. Removing the soft tips before an invasion starts also provides a tasty early crop for the dinner plate. They are young, juicy, fresh and, above all, still 'meat-free' (no one wants the extra protein from blackfly in their food!). The tops can be cooked just like spinach and have a similar texture and appearance, but with that distinctive hint of broad bean flavour.

Taking the tips off broad beans

Easy pest control

The only good thing to come out of the craze for instant garden makeovers was the introduction of water as an essential ingredient of the well-planned garden. For me it is the most relaxing feature in a garden, supplying tranquil sounds, gentle movement and the play of light shimmering on its surface, all calculated to take away the stresses of modern life.

Adding a water feature helps our wildlife in many fascinating ways, too – just watch the action in a natural pond as water skaters skim effortlessly across the surface. The pond on my allotment is the centre of attraction for drinking birds, as well as being a haven for mass-producing the best pest controllers of all – frogs. You know winter's nearly at an end when the first frogspawn appears, and that it's moving on into summer when the tadpoles change into frogs. Then they're off around my plot, polishing off all kinds of vegetable pests for me. Since a frog can live for more than ten years, that's a lot of pests!

Cloches on standby

As I learned long ago, May is one of those nervy months in the garden when we cling to the words of the weather forecaster every evening, hoping against hope not to hear that alarming word 'frost'. It only takes a few days of sunshine for the warming rays to penetrate deep into the soil and stir the earliest sowings into life. A combination of damp soil and rising temperatures quickly brings some surprises to the bare surface. But then they are at real risk, and that's when a few cloches can save the day. If I find early batches of carrots and beetroot have emerged at this time of year, I like to cover them with a cloche. That should protect them and will also bring them on a bit quicker.

Target needy plants

For all my concern with frost this month, May can also bring hot dry weather. Then many gardeners worry about the effects of water deficiency on their plants, often a needless concern as many adapt better than we think to heat and drought.

Everyone loves a lush green lawn, for example, but I despair at times when I see countless gallons of precious water being wasted in an attempt to keep it in pristine condition. Yes, it looks very nice, but even after a prolonged dry spell parched grass soon perks up and returns to its normal condition when the first rains fall. Many shrubs, too, have a deep root system once they are well established, which forages deep underground in search of moisture to satisfy their thirst.

So be selective with water when it is in short supply, and reserve it to give to transplants and seedlings and help them on their way to self-sufficiency. It's better to soak these on a weekly basis than to tease them with small sprinkles daily.

And don't panic! Nature and the British climate have ways of balancing out through time. Gardeners are a philosophical and adaptable race, well up to accepting the challenge of the changing seasons that makes gardening an exciting hobby.

IN THE GREENHOUSE

With the last of the early outdoor plants evicted to the cold frame for hardening off, I can finally bring my greenhouse into action for its summer use.

Tomatoes . . .

The tomatoes are ready to be planted directly into the well-rotted manure and good compost of the borders. I place each tomato plant at the base of a cane angled at about thirty degrees from vertical. This allows the fruit to grow clear of the lush green growth, and the fruit trusses will receive plenty of sunlight to help ripen them.

I grow a range of different tomatoes, including the prolific and well-established greenhouse variety 'Shirley'; a couple of 'Gardener's Delight', still one of the best cherry toms; at least one large beefsteak kind; and one or two of a new variety for trial, such as the large very dark-skinned 'Black Krim'. It's amazing the wide range of different flavours these can produce.

. . . cucumbers . . .

I grow my cucumbers in each corner of the greenhouse, which gives them the warmest positions in the house, with freedom from cool draughts and the highest humidity, exactly the conditions they enjoy. In this way it's possible to have tomatoes and cucumbers with their different needs sharing the same greenhouse.

One variety I tried recently was a novelty to me, a completely round yellow kind called 'Crystal Lemon'. I love trying out the occasional new variety of a vegetable while still retaining some of my favourites. In this way I can explore further afield and experience new or different flavours, but if I don't like them I still have my familiar stalwarts to fall back on.

Like the tomatoes, cucumber plants need canes for support because they grow right up to the roof of the greenhouse, where I string wires across to support their trailing stems. Their long, green torpedoes can then hang down perfectly straight and easy to harvest. Whereas tomatoes have all their sideshoots removed as they grow, I allow each cucumber lateral to run free, only pinching out its tip after a single cucumber has formed.

'Crystal Lemon' cucumbers

... and peppers

The only crop left then to raise in my greenhouse border is sweet peppers. These are slow to grow: sown in March, they seem to take an age to make decent-size plants ready for setting out in the border. But patience is a virtue, and before the end of May they are usually ready to transplant and complete my greenhouse trio of summer salad crops. They are joined in the border by a couple of aubergine plants, which will make a change to my usual diet of vegetables.

The border will then be full, except for the marigolds I always tuck among the crops as companion plants.

Good companions

Companion planting is one technique I've never had much success with, on the open plot at least. Planting carrots among onions to camouflage them from the carrot root fly doesn't seem to work on our hillside. Interspersing aromatic herbs within various crops also fails to deter the various pests that like to thrive on my vegetables.

Where I am more successful is in the enclosed confines of the greenhouse. Among my tomatoes, peppers and cucumbers I plant French marigolds. Their strong aroma in the warm humid atmosphere under glass does keep greenhouse whitefly at bay. As you brush past the marigolds in the borders they release that distinctive smell that always confuses the pests that would otherwise take up residence in the comfort of the greenhouse. On opening the greenhouse door first thing in the morning the pungent smell can be almost overwhelming – no wonder aphids run a mile!

Bean building time

On the plot there is the distinctive sound of bamboo. No! Not the growing variety but the canes going up everywhere to support runner beans and climbing French beans. These make natural 'fences' on the plot, so you must be careful where you site them or they'll cast shadows over some of your sun-loving plants.

It's rapidly approaching the time when the bean plants hardening off in the cold frame need setting out at the base of their canes to start twirling their way up to the top, then loading themselves with tender, tasty green beans. These must be the best crop on the allotment for productivity per square foot, and will continue supplying my dinner table for several months fresh, as well as helping to fill the freezer for use during the more barren winter months.

Those runner bean seeds sown as little as two weeks ago have been planted in warm polystyrene cups that once held office tea and coffee, and their large seed leaves are now filling out. The central shoot is starting to appear and will soon be seeking something to twine round. If I don't liberate them among their bamboo supports they'll wrap themselves into a tangled mess of stems and foliage. Be patient just a little longer, my beauties, and you shall be free!

Tying bean canes

The canes are up and securely fastened to their straining wire in my own unique way. A continuous length of stout string loops them all together and this will hold secure should a summer breeze coast down the valley. But for now, while nights are still cool, the runners and their near relatives, the climbing French bean, are still safely housed in a cold frame to toughen them up ready for their venture into the open plot.

When the time comes later this month I'll place one bean at the base of each cane, and then – to make a super wall of beans and a really bumper crop – one bean plant is added between each pair of canes. The extra bean has no obvious support, so can please itself which cane to climb. This thickens up the row and increases the yield. The trench was well prepared and full of good nutrients, and my feeding regime will ensure they don't suffer from overcrowding.

Many people tie each bean stem to its cane to help it in its quest skyward. I just twist it round the cane to start it on its way, and then leave it alone. Beware, though: in the northern hemisphere a runner bean winds anti-clockwise round the cane and doesn't take kindly to being twisted the wrong way. It will soon unravel again and flap in the breeze.

Carrot maincrop

The sowing season for those young bunching carrots is a long one, from March through to July or later, and just as well: I can think of no other vegetable that can be enjoyed in so many guises. There is nothing crunchier or tastier than a long, slender carrot pulled from its home in the soil, washed well and then eaten raw. A grated carrot adds a colourful dimension and unique flavour to a nice salad. But most of all they are (in my wife's words) the saviour of a cooked meal, providing a vibrant orange colour to what might otherwise look a drab dish. May is the time to sow the maincrop, large store carrots, a key ingredient of every winter stew. The warmer, moister soil this month is perfect for the seeds, and I follow the same procedures as for the earlier April sowing (see pages 94–5).

Potato cover-up

Any early potatoes starting to push their large leaves through the surface could be exposed to frost and wind chill if May is cold. Only a few short weeks ago I was planting them with my mattock, and they'll be in for a shock when they see it back in my hand now. I know what the old plough-horse must have felt like as I draw this between the rows, burying the potato shoots back under a few inches of soil. It is in their best interest and they will be safer underground for a little longer.

This earthing up, to use the technical term, serves many purposes in addition to keeping them snug. It makes more roots on the stem, and

Combat climate change

After a winter as cold as that of 2010/11 it is hard to accept so much evidence from elsewhere for global warming. But, like scientists, many plot-holders believe it is happening and are planting accordingly as an insurance, whether it is almonds and olives, which should appreciate a warmer climate, or willows for fuel and carbon 'capture'.

It is now believed that the humble bamboo does more than any other plant to help reduce the effect of too much carbon dioxide in the atmosphere, and can also generate up to thirty-five per cent more oxygen than most other trees. This hardy plant thrives well in this country, withstanding the extremes of the British climate. You need to choose the right kind, though, for some species are rampant growers and need careful management to fit in with the rest of the garden.

To me as a lover of climbing beans of any and every kind, the greatest benefit of bamboo is as a source of free canes to support the bean vines as they head skywards. But if growing bamboo does indeed have a positive effect, however small, in inhibiting climate change then I would certainly find space on the plot for a clump or two. April or May is the time to put them in – unless you use container-grown plants, which can go in at any time of year.

hence more new potatoes; it helps keep the weeds at bay; and finally it prevents the new tubers from going green. It's not a good idea to eat green potatoes as they are poisonous and will not do you any good.

So that's a useful job well done!

Early treat

One crop that relishes warmer than average conditions in May is the strawberry, and in a good year the plants can be laden with small fruits, as much as a month ahead of expectation, with the risk of the crop finishing before the traditional picking time that coincides with Wimbledon. When all the flowers are set I always net my crop, an urgent precaution to prevent marauding birds from taking too many. They always seem to be up earlier in the morning than I am, and feast on these luscious red fruits before I arrive at the plot, depriving me of my strawberry and cream tea.

Sweet pea rescue

My sweet peas are straining skywards now but cannot grip the smooth canes with their tendrils yet, and a little first-aid is required from me. So it's down on my knees with the string, securing the stems to their supports with loose figure-of-eight loops to help them stay upright. I like to grow plenty of sweet peas, as they are a dual-purpose 'crop', attracting beneficial insects to the plot when those first fragrant flowers are in abundance and almost ready for me to cut.

Securing sweet peas

Hydrotherapy

With the days getting perceptibly longer and warmer, greenfly and blackfly are emboldened to move in and multiply – in favourable weather these little blighters breed like crazy and suck the very life out of our crops. It seems there's no peace for a dedicated organic gardener in the quest to produce a bumper harvest.

I find vigilance is the key to controlling them. As soon as I spot a small colony, it's out with my pump-up pressure sprayer. No chemicals, though, just tepid water. I pump it up to full pressure, turn the nozzle to jet, and then spring into action. Directing this powerful jet straight at the clusters of these pests blasts them to the wet ground where they're unable to do the crawl or breast stroke, so promptly drown. It's easy and chemical-free: all you need is a careful aim to solve this menace, and the result is a clean and completely unharmed plant.

Moving out

The first tender plants to leave the safety of my cold frame this month are the courgettes. After being potted on several times into ever-larger pots, they are now a whopping size. The ample space round my gooseberry bush is their regular home, which allows for their wandering habits, and as usual it has been well manured ready for the greedy plants. With great care I liberate them from their pots and firm them into large holes. Three specimens are enough (they produce an enormous crop if treated right) and I usually try two different varieties, such as green 'Nano Verde di Milano' and yellow 'Atena' to give my plate a colourful look all summer long. After a thorough watering to settle them in, a momentary sense of fear can surface – it's only May, after all. So my last job is to pop a couple of large cloches over them to protect them for a week or two, just in case.

Corn on the cob

One of my favourite summer crops, sweetcorn, has usually made nice
sturdy plants by now in deep root-trainers, and I feel secure in planting
these out towards the end of May. A good variety to grow is 'Prelude', an
early to mid-season cropper that hopefully manages to produce well-
packed cobs full of mouth-watering kernels before the season begins
cooling down again. These plants have to be set out in square blocks, rather
than long rows, to make more certain that the pollen from the (male)
tassels at the top of the plant will fall on to the (female) tassels at the base
of the lower leaves, pollinating them and ensuring super cobs. A relatively
rich soil is best for these tall-growing monsters, and if a dry spell comes
along they need watering regularly to guarantee the cobs are really full.

Planning for Christmas

It might seem a little early in the year, but May is the month when I like
to plant out my Brussels sprouts. Despite the spring sunshine I'm already
thinking of my Christmas dinner, and I wouldn't want to be without these
tasty little green buttons in my festive feast – it's a vegetable that is either
loved or loathed, but it ranks high among my favourites. They need a
long time a-growing, but have already made good strong plants in 5-inch
(13 cm) pots, ready to go out this month in their patch of soil. This area is
reserved for all my brassicas, so it has been well limed to help raise its pH
level to slightly alkaline, which the whole cabbage family likes.

It is hard to believe that such a tough customer as a Brussels sprout
plant has so many enemies. On all allotments there are usually plots with
that dreaded fungal disease, club root. This attacks all members of the
brassica family, causing large swellings on the roots that starve the plant of
water and nutrients. My plants have made a good root structure so far in
their pots, but to avoid their coming into contact with the soil I dig a
9-inch (23 cm) hole and line it with a liberal coating of lime. Then I place a

plant in the centre of this large hole and bed it in with good compost. This will help it to make a large root system and get well established before it has to face any threat from club root. Getting sprouts off to the best start in life is the secret of success.

Swedes

Another key member of my winter supply of fresh vegetables is the swede, which needs sowing now, directly into the soil in rows 18 inches (45 cm) apart and half an inch (13 mm) deep. As a member of the brassica clan, swedes need soil limed to make it slightly alkaline, just like sprouts. If you water the seeds well, they should be popping through quickly in six to ten days' time.

In recent years, however, there have been long dry periods after I have sown my swedes, so I have resorted to starting the seeds in compartmental trays. I sow two seeds per module in two trays of twenty-four. I try to end up with forty-eight young swede plants after thinning out the weakest seedlings, and this gives me a good supply of these hardy vegetables right through from October until next April. There is no problem transplanting swede plants and no danger of forked roots, always a risk when transplanting some root crops. Planting out strong, sturdy plants also avoids the damage that flea beetles can inflict on the young leaves of emerging swede seedlings.

With my swede crop under way it only remains to plant out the leeks, which on our allotments is usually best done in June. Then it will just be a matter of waiting patiently for all the key winter vegetables to crop in the coming autumn and winter months.

Looking back

It seems a very long time ago now, but I took on my first plot at the tender age of eleven and, much to the amazement of the older gardeners there, made a success of it. They took me under their wing, freely passing on generations of accumulated knowledge and experience. My young brain absorbed this wealth of information that has stood me in good stead throughout my gardening life.

From that early start I developed an allotment 'empire' in the 1950s when many plots were empty and abandoned, and at one stage was actually cultivating ten full-size plots. As I obviously could not eat all this produce I started selling it, and I believe (though it's never been proved, of course) that I founded the 'box' system for selling vegetables. You were not supposed to sell produce from the allotments, so I cunningly charged for the empty box and 'gave' the vegetables free.

MAY IN A NUTSHELL

Key jobs for MAY

- ✔ Make successional sowings of salad crops.
- ✔ Plant early crops after hardening them off.
- ✔ Net fruits as they start to ripen.
- ✔ Sow winter swedes.
- ✔ Keep weeds at bay.
- ✔ Plant out those climbing beans.

If you have time . . .

- ✔ Clean out the shed to store all the pots and trays emptying this month.

Looking ahead to JUNE

- ✔ Net brassicas to keep off butterflies.
- ✔ Harvest broad beans.
- ✔ Plant cabbages where broad beans have finished.
- ✔ Start a feeding regime to keep crops healthy.

Planting peppers

Thought for the month

My allotment has provided many of my life's basic needs. It is my open air 'gym' where I can tone my muscles with gentle exercise. I can enjoy the fresh air and the warming rays of the sunshine on my skin, providing me with a tan and my daily dose of Vitamin D. It can be a place for solitude and contemplation, or somewhere to relax in social conversation with like-minded gardeners. It is my 'stress counsellor', helping any tensions evaporate with the calming tonic of being at one with my surroundings. Then – the icing on the cake – there's the sheer joy of reaping my own produce, raised in a natural state, free from chemicals and insecticides. These arrive on my plate mere hours after harvesting, releasing that exquisite flavour that can only be experienced when you grow your own.

JUNE

WE ARE INTO THE SIXTH MONTH of the year – the longest day is rapidly approaching, and the greater number of daylight hours gives plants more growing time. The plot, which not so long ago seemed to be a barren, empty piece of earth, is fast disappearing under a canopy of young, fresh, promising growth.

At last all those tender plants that have been lurking in the greenhouse and cold frame can be released into the open ground: this is the time when frost should be a memory and any crop can be sown outdoors without much risk to its health.

Not only are the plants enjoying these perfect growing conditions but the weeds, too, seem to positively relish every moment. Look around you, though – as a gardener you have to admire the hedgerows and road verges now. There are those vivid yellow buttercups and dandelions with their riot of bloom, and golden-eyed daisies making a lake of white as their flowers carpet the banks beside the busy traffic. This is indeed a bold display.

All the wildflowers are alive now with insects, bees and butterflies. Somewhere I was reading with concern that many of our butterflies are in rapid decline. The loss of any species is a major blow to the diversity of animals and plants that make this world such a unique place. So I welcome them all – even the cabbage white!

The tempo of life on the allotments is certainly more relaxed and there is time to stand and stare. I love it!

Enough of this midsummer daydreaming. Whenever I am standing there just looking and watching life all around me, I am quickly brought back to reality when one of our many plot-holders passes by and asks, 'How's the plot faring, then?'

Last month's overall green on the plot is being broken up now by the appearance of flowers here and there, nowhere more so than on the walls of runner beans that have now reached the tops of their canes. Their bright crimson flowers conjure up great expectations that in a few short weeks we will be harvesting those first tender pods.

The runner bean is probably among the most popular of all vegetables because it provides a prolific crop for the smallest amount of ground used. All it needs is very fertile soil and plenty of water to flourish, plus the help of many bumble bees to pollinate its flowers. The pods will then fill your plate throughout the summer and, in addition, help to stock the freezer for those hot winter dinners. There is nothing better than the taste of a runner bean in winter to rekindle pleasant thoughts of the summer past.

And talking of flowers, the giant pumpkin has finally been freed from its polythene corral, and the warmer weather and plenty of seaweed feed have set it romping across the plot. Already some 6 feet (1.8 m) from root to runner tip, it will have the same distance to go before I start looking for the first bright yellow female flower with a tiny pumpkin at its base. Then I will don my bee outfit (!) and pollinate it by hand. All I hope is that both female and male flowers open at the same time.

Pumpkin roaming the plot

Feeding the frogs

At the bottom of the plot where my pond is sited and all around in the nettles and grass surrounding this watery haven, there is the constant movement of little froglets leaving the water and starting their life on land. Like most youngsters, these are looking for food, which is the chance for me to go hunting among my plants and seek out the aphids lurking among the juicy young growth. I collect these pests in a paper bag and scatter them around the pond area.

Frog at pond edge

This rids me of these sucking pests and provides a feast for the froglets, allowing them to grow big and strong, and hopefully then go off hunting on my plot to find the other pests hiding in the dense foliage. The solution for gardener and wildlife alike, and a perfect example of the way we can cohabit with nature.

The thieving blackbird

I normally coexist with our huge bird population quite amicably, but at this time of year we can have a falling out. And what causes this breakdown in our happy relationship? It's the battle of the strawberries. By now these are filling out and making plump, inviting berries, and with the increased sunlight and warmth they will be ripening very soon. The trouble is that the birds which inhabit the hedgerows surrounding my plot enjoy these tasty fruits as much as I do. And the blackbird is the chief culprit. It has a particular liking for these juicy red berries, so it is out with the netting if I am to have any for myself.

Tales from the plot

As the days heated up one June our water butts very quickly ran dry, and it was a case of climbing the mountainside to get our water supply up and running. Albie and I share a hose, so it was into the stream for me to clean out the submerged bucket and fill the hosepipe with water while Albie had the complicated job of keeping his finger over the end of the hose.

The pipe was sunk into the filled bucket and I gave Albie a shout to remove his finger to let gravity do the rest. After two abortive attempts we had success, and the icy cold water was flowing freely out of the pipe once more. Soon all the drums were full and the water warming up in the midday sun.

Albie decided to sprinkle fertilizer round his plants, and then turned on his hosepipe to water it in. Suddenly there was this plaintive cry from his plot: 'Terry, the water has stopped again!'

It was off up the mountain slopes once more to find the cause, and there in our bucket was a huge pile of silt. I soon cleaned this out, but try as I might I could not get the water flowing again. I summoned the help of Carl and together we pushed wires down the pipe, shook it, banged it, but all to no avail. So we decided we would have to split the long run of hosepipe to find the blockage, and that way we found part of the problem and removed the silt from the pipe. Still it would not run.

All this time Albie was standing on his plot with one finger over the open end of the pipe. In sheer desperation I shouted down the mountain, 'Remove your finger while I blow through the pipe.' This he duly did, but I did not realize he was still staring down the open end of the pipe. I gave a great blow and suddenly the blockage was dislodged. Then there was an almighty yell as all the silt and debris, together with a large build-up of water, soaked him from head to toe.

A neighbour of mine had some work done that required scaffolding. On completion the builder said he did not need all the scaffolding poles back. Cut into 8-foot (2.4 m) lengths, they would be perfect as bean poles. There were nine of them and all I had to do was collect them, so I struck a deal with Dave H, as he had a truck, and they were soon on the way to the allotment. The deal was three for Dave, three for me and somehow Albie got in on the deal and got the other three.

This unexpected windfall means that next year I can build a new place to grow my beans and leave the existing poles in place – moving these year on year is such a chore that it never happens and my beans end up growing in the same spot. Now those few poles have brought a whole new dimension to my plot as I can rotate the beans with a minimum of fuss.

One Sunday when I arrived at the allotments, Albie was busily watering away. I said, 'Why are you doing that when there is heavy rain forecast this afternoon?'

'That won't happen,' he replied.

Then Tony and Ron came through the gate, and the same conversation took place.

Shortly afterwards Terry S came over from the far side of the allotments and said to Albie, 'I'm leaving before it rains!'

'That will never happen,' Albie said.

Eventually we all went home, happy in the knowledge that rain would fall later in the day and save us the work. Needless to say, not a drop fell on our valley hillside, and as we all turned up the next day Albie had that smug look on his face as if to say, 'I told you so!'

So look out Derek Brockway, your job as BBC weather forecaster to the Rhondda valleys is in jeopardy! You can always rely on a local lad with local knowledge, especially when he lives less than a hundred yards from the allotment.

The heat of the afternoon was a perfect invitation for me to don my shorts (not a pretty sight at the best of times), put on my sun hat and remove the hoe from my shed. I could almost see the weeds quake as I walked purposefully down the path. With a rhythmic to and fro action it was an easy task to sever these young weeds from their roots, and the scorching afternoon sun did the rest as they withered up in the heat. This is the easy approach to ridding the plot of weeds and a perfect way to spend a sunny afternoon.

Then one weekend, what happened? Just as I thought hot June had well and truly set in, the mercury plummeted down the thermometer and the temperature was back in single figures. On the Friday evening it started to rain steadily, this only days after I had started up my irrigation system to water my brassicas. All through the night it rained, and at heart I was grateful for the quenching stuff falling from the skies.

But by Saturday afternoon the skies darkened further and became more threatening, and then the show really started. Crazy, silvery lightning bolts darted across the black skies with momentary vivid flashes that eerily illuminated the dark valley, followed by a crescendo of noise as great thunder claps rolled above my head. The rain turned into a monsoon, falling straight as stair rods from the sinister clouds, and within minutes there was 'water, water everywhere'.

The summer storm moved after an hour or so, but the heavy rain continued falling for some time. We needed a drop of rain but not a deluge. Still, those wilting Brussels sprouts must have been happy!

In my entire half-century or more on this allotment there has never been a rabbit inside the gates. Until the other weekend, that is, just when our young crops were at their most tender and toothsome. One of our tenants was on his plot at the crack of dawn and spotted them nibbling the tops of his young runner beans.

Now gardeners are mostly in tune with the creatures of nature, living alongside them in a degree of peace and harmony – yes, even slugs and snails! But a family of rabbits and an allotment simply don't mix. They are difficult to coexist with as they flit from plant to plant stealing the juicy growing tips.

Immediately there were hasty discussions of what we could do to scare them away. We were hoping they were just temporarily lost and only passing through, because they were certainly not welcome guests (happily they got the message and eventually disappeared again).

One thing about life on an allotment is that little or nothing changes quickly. A lot of us on the plots have been gardening here since the Ice Age, it seems. Many have spent thirty or forty years plus on this very site, and there are times as we share a coffee break together that we start reminiscing and digging deep into our ageing memories.

There are pleasant recollections of allotmenteers of years ago and what we learned from them, and there are those classic moments to recall when old-timers passed on valuable tips, many of which are still acted upon by us gardening there today. The time will surely come when we in our turn will pass on this lore to new up-and-coming gardeners, and so the knowledge will be saved for perpetuity. Secrets should not die with old gardeners.

All our crops now seem to be making hay while the sun shines, putting on growth fast as the extended days supply the light needed for photosynthesis to occur. This technical term lies at the heart of life itself, and is the process by which a plant produces food using the green pigment in its leaves. Plants behave differently from us mortals, taking in carbon dioxide and using the sunlight to convert it to sugars, and then give off as a by-product the life-giving oxygen we need. What a clever system of coexistence between man and plant for mutual benefit – not only do plants provide us with the food we eat, they provide the pure air we breathe. As more and more carbon dioxide is pumped out to pollute the atmosphere, perhaps we should cultivate more plants on our plots to redress the balance!

I really must learn to say 'No!' when I am offered orphaned plants, but the trouble is I don't have it in my heart to turn them away. Only the other day Gary had a spare pumpkin plant looking for a home, and as usual I willingly accepted it. But then came the dilemma of where to plant it as my plot was already full and bursting at the seams. A rapid think and then the plastic sheet came off the top of my compost heap to provide the forlorn plant with a new home. I hope it likes it there with that great store of goodness at its roots, and that I will get a bountiful harvest of pumpkins as a reward.

One year disaster struck, and in my greenhouse of all places! The previous autumn I was given a lorryload of well-rotted manure from a friend of a friend. It looked super stuff, but never judge a gift by its look and smell.

I prepared my greenhouse border in the usual way, working in lashings of this black gold. On my return from holiday, however, there were distorted, grotesquely twisted plants sticking out of the soil where my prize tomatoes should have been, and it turned out that my tomatoes had been poisoned by herbicide residues lurking in the manure. This was an unexpected silent killer.

Since then this problem with manure has been well publicized. Farmers spray their grass meadows with this herbicide to kill off the weeds, but the weedkiller is still present in the hay fed to horses and takes a considerable time to break down into a harmless substance.

When will we ever learn that man-made chemicals are harmful to the environment, especially if we have no idea of their long-term effects? Nature can take care of itself and has done for millions of years, so why does man need to interfere with that process? We inevitably suffer the consequences and sometimes pay heavily for this recklessness.

PLOT PROGRESS

If you have to miss a week on the plot through some awful weather (June is not always flaming these days!), the change in the landscape may seem dramatic on your return, and it can take a trained eye to spot even a glimpse of dark brown earth on the plot. Green foliage extends everywhere, broken up perhaps by the vivid dark reds of beetroot with 'Lollo Rosso' lettuce almost blood red in contrast. Occasionally there are little white or purple flowers standing proud above the masses of thriving potato foliage punctuating this massed green display. But the sight that gladdens the eye of most gardeners is the majestic crimson flowers adorning the long flower stalks amongst the runner beans. Even in unseasonable conditions most plants fare well this month and are moving on to maturity, a sign that summer has truly arrived.

Payback time

The daily tasks are changing, too, as more time is diverted from sowing and planting to a routine of daily harvesting. Yes, it is payback time on the plot!

What more exciting moment in gardening can there be than to plunge a fork into the ground near a full-grown potato plant and discover a crop? At this stage the results are completely unknown. But the moment the root comes out of the soil, one shake and those brilliant white tubers fall like a hailstorm on to the ground. Truly worth waiting for!

Lifting this crop can make some much-needed room available on the packed plot for a new sowing, in this case a quick-maturing salad crop that will appreciate its new home in the fine fertile soil.

As you walk the plot more surprises may hit you. The fern-like tops of carrots, maybe hiding a new treasure below the soil: one tug on this foliage and out of the ground (hopefully) slips the long, tapered orange root of one of our more colourful vegetables. One step further, and the firm heart of a cabbage may await your attention. Another small step, and there in clusters hang pods of broad beans – pop open a pod, and there, nestling in the furry chamber, are the first small oval beans.

This walk around the plot can supply the makings of a superb fresh summer meal, with only a joint of meat and some tasty gravy needed to complete a wholesome feast of delight. And there will be more to come as other crops reach their harvest time. Even in a season marked by a lack of high summer sunshine, there is usually a beam on my face as the time of plenty brings joy from the plot to the kitchen.

Look after the bees

By now warmth and long days have usually created a strongly scented wall of beautiful sweet-pea blooms, and my wife is always very happy to receive her daily bouquet of these, the most wonderful of flowers. I get a great sensual feeling of peace in the cool of the evening while cutting these headily scented blooms – this to me is one of the most relaxing jobs on the plot, and I am sure it is the delicate perfume of the flowers that helps me unwind.

Bees love them almost as much as I do. I am a great fan of our greatest ally, the bee, a godsend for gardeners if our crops and fruit are to produce bumper harvests. With this in mind I try to poach as many bees as I can and lure them to my plants, and for this I sow poached-egg plants (*Limnanthes douglasii*) all around the edges of the plot. With their brilliant yellow centres and white frilly edges, they look superb in the sunshine, but as well as looking pretty they are always awash with bees of all denominations. My hope is that while the bees are there they will venture off to the rest of the plot and have a change of diet on some of my other crops. If this fails then I will have to appeal to Bill Turnbull (the BBC newsreader who is also a well-known bee-keeper) for a hive or two of his bees!

Follow the trail

Perhaps my favourite vegetable of all is green peas, and the first are ready this month. There is nothing better than picking a few of the packed pods and popping them as you toil away, munching on the fresh raw peas that are so much healthier than a packet of sweets and many times tastier.

They are also great memory joggers for an ancient forgetful gardener. Life on a busy allotment site inevitably includes a fresh brew and a few minutes of sociable conversation now and again. The problem is that when I get back to work, I have often forgotten where I stopped. No problem, though, if there is a trail of empty pea pods to help me retrace my steps. Now, if I could only find an equally simple way of remembering where I put down tools when I have been distracted!

The first peas!

Crop maintenance

My tomato plants are usually reaching for the stars by now, with the first trusses of fruit forming as little green balls. This is a sign that the feeding regime needs to commence. Seaweed extract is my preferred fertilizer, and I use this solution to feed the plants at least three times per week. And on my daily excursions into the greenhouse I give the canes supporting the tomatoes a sharp tap – I swear by this and believe it helps the flowers set fruit.

From now on those tomato plants need checking regularly for the little growths that appear at the leaf nodes. Removing these sideshoots with finger and thumb while they are still small helps make a compact plant that concentrates on putting all its energies into producing a crop. I don't do this with cherry-type varieties, though, as bushy plants provide many more of these small, red tomatoes.

My cucumbers are also running wild up their canes now, and it is a daily job to secure the rapidly growing main stems, tie in the fruiting laterals and remove any new growth beyond the first cucumber to form on each sideshoot. Already lots of small cucumbers are apparent along the stems. With these and the tomatoes coming on so strongly I make a point of leaving the side windows of the greenhouse constantly open at this time of year to provide good ventilation. This helps prevent the atmosphere from becoming too steamy and providing an ideal place for blight and other fungal diseases to thrive.

Filling the salad bowl

As well as sowing lettuces regularly for a constant supply, I need a succession of spring onions and radishes to complete my salad selection. Again it is all about sowing little and often, which I don't do out on the plot despite having a large allotment: I feel I have greater control over continuity by keeping the plants in containers.

I have a number of florist's buckets with holes drilled in the bottom for drainage, and I use these for sowing my spring onions and radishes in small amounts. I fill two buckets with compost and sow one with the radishes, the other with the onions. When these are growing well, I start another pair of buckets. By adjusting the timing according to weather and time of year, it is possible to have an ample supply of fresh salad crops all summer.

Sowing spring onions and radishes in buckets

Liming beans

Those first flowers are forming on the runner beans this month, and the plants need all the nutrients they can muster from the soil to help the first flowers set and form those tender young pods – otherwise they have a tendency to drop off and leave a carpet of flowers on the ground. The soil has been fed well but all these soil-borne nutrients need to be quickly absorbed by the plants. To this end I add a handful of hydrated lime to my 2-gallon (10-litre) watering can, stir it well to make a creamy mix, and then use this to soak the roots of the vigorous young plants. This makes the nutrients more easily available to their roots and encourages early pods at the bottom of the plant. I do this twice a week until the lower flowers are set and small beans are hanging there.

Mulch for moisture

If the previous few weeks have been very dry, there might be a long, hot, dry summer in prospect. Now is a good time to help conserve the precious moisture in the soil by applying a thick coating of good mulch from my wormeries and the contents of my green plastic compost bins. I use this mainly among my rows of runner beans, and after giving them a good watering I spread the mulch thickly around the roots to help reduce evaporation. This also reinforces the soil's fertility, and my twice-weekly liquid feeds pass straight through, adding to the food store these hungry crops have to draw on.

Food for growth

I depend on my wormeries for feeding my crops during this period of rapid growth as they can provide lots of rich, dark organic nutrients, and this 'live' food is also full of micro-organisms which invigorate the soil around the roots. My drum of sheep manure (see page 75) is also very high in nitrogen, and a cupful of this liquid added to a canful of water is just the tonic the crops need. This feeding regime needs to be short and sharp, just long enough to sustain all that vigorous growth, but should cease in August so that there is not too much tender new foliage left to face the hardships of the ensuing colder weather.

My compost sandwich

Weeding is a regular task this time of the year when crops need every inch of ground to themselves, and that is good news for my composting process. I have always composted all the green waste coming off the plot, and throughout the summer months I produce the 'McWalton' sandwich. This is built up with 5-inch (12 cm) layers of green waste alternated with 10-inch (20 cm) layers of well-rotted horse manure. I build this compost heap during the summer months when the plot is producing masses of weeds and vegetable waste. During the winter I cover the finished heap with black polythene, and by spring I have a perfect supply of material to work back into the plot. In addition I have a series of green 'Dalek' composting bins for household and kitchen waste, interspersed with the lawn grass.

Composting has always been a subject close to my heart. When I began allotment gardening in the 1950s one of my regular summertime tasks was to collect bracken from the surrounding hillsides. This rotted down into perfect compost and, supplemented with horse manure from the local colliery where the pit ponies were kept, was the perfect organic way to keep the plot in good heart. But times changed, the colliery closed down, and collecting bracken became a time-consuming task. Nothing is for ever, and now I reckon making your own compost with weeds and waste is the best way.

Harvesting green garlic

By now my garlic from last year's crop has usually gone rather soft – it has been nearly a year in store, after all – so it is time to think about adding some fresh garlic to the ingredients for my wife's dishes. There is no need to allow this year's growing garlic to die back before harvesting can start, and freshly lifted green garlic is wonderful. So it's out with the hand fork to ease a bulb from the soil, and there you have it, the perfect flavour enhancer. I will continue to use the fresh garlic while it is still growing until it eventually dies back, when it is ready to dry for storage and use all winter. There's no call to buy what you have at hand, growing on the plot. Which reminds me, my first turnips are ready in June, so that adds yet another dimension to my dinner plate. Truly, variety is the spice of life and never more so than on a vegetable plot.

Harvesting green garlic

Rogues gallery of pests

Although not quite feast time for us yet, all the young growth is a magnet for marauding pests cruising the skies looking for a tasty fresh meal. Being an organic gardener, I have to rely on vigilance and, where possible, protection for the crops, rather than reaching for the spray gun. Let's take a look at some of the nasties lurking out there waiting to feed on the fruits of our labour.

Take the humble but robust cabbage, which you might think is practically indestructible. This vegetable has more enemies than any other. The tender foliage attracts the grey mealy bug, which feeds on the sap, makes the foliage go red and green, and eventually sucks the very life out of the plant. Below ground its roots are being devoured by the maggots of the cabbage root fly, which eats up the entire root, killing the plant by stopping it taking up water and nutrients from the ground.

If the cabbage shrugs off these pests, along comes the pretty little cabbage white butterfly which lays its eggs on the underside of the leaves. These hatch and the caterpillars then strip the plant of all its foliage, leaving nothing for us. Do not despair though: help is at hand. Simply cover the plants with a fine mesh, supported by a framework of battens nailed together – an effective addition to my other defences: my rhubarb brew (see page 56) and, to ward off the cabbage root fly, my plastic collars (see page 72).

The sworn enemy of carrot lovers is also flying about looking for a place to lay its eggs. This month the carrot root fly is on the wing. The maggots of this pest feed on the newly forming carrots, filling them with holes and making them unfit for our consumption. However, it seems that the carrot root fly cannot fly more than about 21 inches (52 cm) above the ground – a sufferer of vertigo, I suppose – so a screen of mesh this high around plants is an effective barrier.

The other major pests on all tender growth on plants are the prodigious aphids. The only answer to these in the organic world is to crush them with your fingers or to blast them off the plants with a pressure sprayer filled with tepid water (they are not good swimmers).

Do not be put off by this constant battle: winning it gives you tasty, insecticide-free, wholesome food.

Reaching for the skies

Nowhere is competition more evident in the plant world than among those vegetables that grow heavenwards. It is very obvious with runner beans and climbing French beans, which seem to wind their way up at a fantastic pace in their quest to reach the top of their canes before their neighbours. On every visit to the plot they always seem so much taller than the previous time.

But in their race to reach the sky some lose their grip, and you find their leading shoot is flapping in the breeze frantically trying to regain its hold. This is when they need a hand. Simply twirl it back around the stick, but take note: the runner bean twines anti-clockwise, and any attempt to make it do otherwise causes confusion and it will soon be back waving in the wind again, only this time quite a bit longer. Everything in nature has little quirks – like ourselves, when you think about it.

Watering *is* worthwhile

Watering is one of those jobs I call a chore as it is forced on a gardener by the weather, but your plants often need it. How you do it is very important: it's no good sprinkling small amounts of water around the crops, for example, as this only teases them. If it is to be done properly, ensure they get a really good soak.

I have a regime on the plot during dry periods to make certain the water is used most beneficially, and gets right down to the roots. I divide my plot into three parts, and then water each in turn, one a day, so that there is a three-day interval between soakings in each area. This makes the task easier and less

The worst weed of all

So what is a weed? To an experienced gardener it is quite simply a plant in the wrong place, which might be a bright flowering border plant that is not there by design and ruins your aesthetic plan. To me the most annoying weed is the potato. When you replant last year's potato patch with some other small-growing vegetable, this overlooked monster pushes its way to the surface and thrusts the new arrivals out of the way. Removing its little old tuber defies all attempts and half your row of seedlings is soon disturbed. You dig and dig down into the earth trying to trace it and when you finally find it, it is no bigger than a marble. This little potato has survived several diggings and forkings, a whole winter in the soil, and yet still grows. The mayhem and havoc it causes make it a real weed to me!

tedious, and ensures all get their fair share. A little liquid feed added to the watering can also helps plants through the stressful time of day when temperatures can rise into the high 20s Celsius. Remember, a healthy plant is a happy plant, and better able to cope with attacks from pests and diseases.

Don't forget the leeks!

Before all my ground is finally filled I need to plant out that most Welsh of crops, my leeks. Timing these is critical: plant too early and they bolt in September, plant too late and there will be no fat leeks for the pot. Mid-June on our hillside is historically the best time, and gardening is all about what works for you.

The seeds were sown way back in March, pricked out into seed trays in mid-April, and are now the thickness of pencils, just right for their move into the ground. I pull them out of the compost, bare-rooted, and trim about half an inch (13 mm) from both their roots and their green leaf tips with sharp scissors – this shocks the seedlings and makes transplanting more successful.

To plant these I use a crowbar (left over from my old night-time job). After unwinding a tight string line across the plot, I make holes with the crowbar every 4 inches (10 cm), deep enough to leave about 1½ inches (4 cm) of green leaf tip above the soil. If you are not confident about making the holes to the correct depth, put an elastic band tightly around the bar to mark how far to drive it in.

I pop a leek in each hole, but do not refill it with soil, just flood it with water to bed the roots in, then let the holes fill in by themselves over time while the portion of leek below ground swells and develops into the tastiest white part. To increase the length of the blanch, I will in a few weeks' time slip an opaque plastic sleeve over each plant, when it is about 12 inches (30 cm) tall and still spindly.

Try something different

Late June is a good time to experiment with a few new crops, once all the basic crops are in and are growing well. As you harvest broad beans and early potatoes, patches of rich ground become available, so let's not waste them and leave them idle. There is a range of vegetables that fit the bill and give you some new pleasurable flavours to sample.

Corn salad (perhaps better known as lamb's lettuce), chicory, Florence fennel and pak choi are very suitable for these empty spaces. They are all vegetables that need to grow unchecked by wild variations in temperature and are particularly adapted to the summer months. Sown too early, they readily bolt to seed and will be useless; sow now, though, and they will be ready to harvest in the autumn.

Also readily available in catalogues and garden centres these days are quick-maturing baby vegetables such as carrots and beetroot that can be ready to harvest just ten to twelve weeks after sowing. Pop a few short rows of these in and they too will give you extra vegetables as autumn approaches, making the plot even more productive, especially if you keep the soil well-fed. The rewards can be great!

Looking back

When I look at my plot a significant difference between now and years ago springs to mind. I seem now to have miles of barrier protection that I have to erect to keep marauding pests from feasting on my crops. The cabbages are covered with netting to stop those fluttering butterflies laying their eggs on my lush green plants and devouring all in a few short days. The carrots are covered with Enviromesh to prevent silent, secretive carrot flies from laying eggs among that ferny foliage, their young descending deep into the soil to devour my long, orange roots. And the strawberries are netted to keep out those birds that are up before me in the morning, breakfasting on all my delicious red berries.

In my early days as a gardener on these very allotments years ago none of this was needed. There must have been a better balance in those days between pest and predator, with the equilibrium tilted in favour of the predators. What has changed to destroy this delicate balance? Modern life, insecticides, chemicals must have moved us on to an era where war with pests is a daily battle, and protection has become the main weapon to use if we are to remain true to organic principles.

On a more positive note, though, our allotments used to be an all-male domain, with mostly retired men filling their time growing vegetables. But in the past ten years the place has improved with the influence of a female touch as more wives join their husbands there. My wife often comes along and so does Brian's, while Julie even has a plot of her own. The latest convert is the wife of a newer member, Tony: she has donned an apron and is right in there with him, helping out on the plot. This is great to see and helps bring a new dimension to our allotment.

JUNE IN A NUTSHELL

Key jobs for JUNE

- Start lifting early potatoes.
- Plant out leeks when pencil-size.
- Reuse cropped spaces for late sowings of vegetables such as pak choi and Florence fennel.
- Net strawberries to keep out hungry birds.
- Remove sideshoots from tomatoes.
- Tie cucumbers to supports.

If you have time . . .

- Plant flowers among your crops to attract pollinators.

Looking ahead to JULY

- Remove harvested bean tops and interplant with a catch crop of brassicas.
- Clean and remove foliage from strawberry bed.
- Feed those hungry bean crops.
- Keep pests at bay with daily vigilance and inspection.
- Harvest garlic.

Blasting greenfly off runner beans

Thought for the month

How I love these balmy June nights! Having spent many hours of the day weeding, planting or socializing on the allotment, it is great to return late in the evening after feasting on my own produce, and just sit and look at the plot. I always rest on the step by my greenhouse, and there I can survey the whole of my little piece of Paradise. As the poet asks, 'What is this life if, full of care / We have no time to stand and stare?' Very apt on a busy allotment.

The backdrops to the plot are the lovely wooded hillsides of the Rhondda valley, which at this time of year are a verdant green. I wonder sometimes at the changes that have occurred in this former mining valley, where the hillsides have been reclaimed from the black slag heaps and restored to their previous splendour of hundreds of years ago. In my small lifetime on this allotment I have experienced many of these changes at first hand, and I am eternally grateful for the privilege of witnessing nature reclaim her own.

JULY

JULY IS A LOVELY TIME ON THE ALLOTMENTS. The workload is diminishing, everything growing on the plot seems to be striving to outdo its neighbours, and there are the bountiful daily harvests to collect.

To me this is high summer, and the stream of carrier bags leaving the plot stands testimony to the plentiful crops arriving in my kitchen. Almost every meal now comes from the plot, the freezer is rapidly filling with my winter stores, and there is some produce spare to share with friends and neighbours.

The hot nights and humidity can send all the plants into overdrive as they rush headlong to make lots of growth. Squashes, marrows and, best of all, the courgettes are laden with little green fruits filling out before my eyes, and already there could be a glut looming on the horizon. I hope my wife has the recipe book at the ready as these are turned into all sorts of dishes including courgette cake with a delicious distinctive taste that goes down well with a cup of tea.

This is the peak fruit harvest, with large dishes of redcurrants, raspberries, blackcurrants and gooseberries being collected up and down the plots. It is like a good old pick-your-own farm as everyone trades the various types of fruits, but only if you are prepared to pick them yourself.

It isn't sunshine all the way during July, of course, especially on our valley allotments, and many a day I have had to shelter from the rain pouring down steadily with a stiff breeze blowing behind it. But this is Wales, a land full of reservoirs and bright green rolling hillsides. You don't get that beautiful scenery without a spot or two of rain.

Crops to share and sample

As the period of crop harvesting gets under way, very often there is an unexpected surplus. Some of this can be stored or frozen, but much has to be used swiftly, and this is when swapping and bartering transactions begin to take place on the allotments as plot-holders share out this excess produce.

Despite the potential of a full-size plot, it is not possible to grow the entire range of all the diverse vegetables that are available. Most of my patch is used for family favourites, but like most other allotmenteers I like to try something new each year. These unusual vegetables are often shared out across the plots, offering everyone the opportunity to experience some new tastes. If they are to your liking, then another packet of seeds may be on your shopping list for next year; if not, then at least you tried and need never bother with them again. Gardening on an allotment site can offer access to a wider range of vegetables than may be grown by your own fair hand.

The trouble with rain

The amounts of rain falling on my allotment are sometimes very high – not for nothing is Wales a land of rivers and waterfalls. This might reduce the need to water crops during summer, but there may be a penalty to pay.

I always dig plenty of good humus material into the plot over winter, both to maintain fertility and also to hold moisture. The second reason is obviously unnecessary in a really wet season, but constant downpours also leach a lot of the added nutrients from my soil. Faltering growth and yellowing leaves on crops are often an indication of hunger in a wet season.

Many years ago we would have reached out for artificial fertilizers to replace these lost nutrients. A dressing of sulphate of ammonia would have given a quick nitrogen boost, superphosphate would help the bean population flourish, while for 'lazy' gardeners a scattering of Growmore would have covered all these various needs.

No more of these quick fixes for me, though. To help replace some of the nutrient losses from heavy rain I apply a 50:50 mixture of concentrated manure and blood, fish and bone, which I scatter over the ground in the wet conditions to help the ground to absorb it quickly. The manure gives the growing plants a speedy boost while the blood, fish and bone breaks down more slowly, feeding growth over a longer period. As a liquid feed these days I generally use seaweed extract.

Back in my early days on the site, many of the homes in this mining village had coal fires. This gave chimney sweeps a regular job, and the allotments were an obvious final home for the resultant soot – if weathered for about a year, it makes a good nitrogenous feed and is a great soil improver for bean and pea crops. Alternatively it can be steeped in water like the sheep manure.

Predators to the rescue

While rummaging among crops to find something to harvest, keep a lookout for pests and, even more importantly, for those insects which are our allies. This time of year pests have access to plenty of feed sites and their populations increase rapidly. But their numbers supply the food source for our allies, which also start to multiply.

One of the most voracious aphid predators among these allies is the ladybird, an odd-looking beetle with its bright red body and prominent black spots. The adult might be beautiful and easy to identify, but its larvae are not so attractive and can be easily mistaken for a pest. They are grey and mottled, and look for all the world like miniature crocodiles. Their sole diet is sap-sucking aphids, which they scoff in large quantities for about three weeks before changing into the beautiful adults – and these, too, continue eating aphids for the rest of their days.

Tales from the plot

Despite the incessant rain, harvesting was well under way on the now fully productive plots when 'Bolts' came down the path bearing a fresh cabbage he had just cut. He was proud of his large specimen and could not resist showing it to the assembled gathering sheltering on the coffee bench. I imagine he expected praise, but he had come to the wrong place and was quickly brought back to earth by comments such as 'You'd be better putting that on the compost heap rather than taking it home.' But despite the put-down he went off carrying his prize cabbage in triumph in the rain, and I bet it made a fine addition to his dinner.

Just then John P arrived with an unusual plant he had bought in a local store.

'What have you got there, then?' we asked.

'A kiwi-fruit bush,' he replied.

We all looked at the label and said, 'Well, you can't plant that here.'

'Why not?' he protested.

'It says to plant in a sunny position. So where are you going to find that this summer?'

There is always a quip or two flying around the plots, and that is what makes it such a happy place to be, whatever the weather.

I would not believe that the mobile phone could be an essential part of the gardener's tool kit. There I was, sitting in Albie's café, when his mobile rang: it was Bob calling from the other side of the allotments enquiring what everyone was doing about lunch. Whatever has happened to those good old days when a shout across the plots would suffice or even, for those fitter young things, a stroll over to communicate face to face with your fellow gardeners? What changes technology is making even in the simple world of the allotments!

I was very fortunate recently to have my four-year-old granddaughter staying with us and accompanying me to the allotments. As I walked in through the gates with her holding my hand tightly, memories of my own young days came flooding back. I was exactly the same age as her when my father took me along to his plot, and those first vivid memories have remained with me forever.

She was in awe of all the plants growing there and bombarded me with many questions.

'What are those things growing there, Pop-Pops [her name for me]?' she asked.

'They're carrots,' I replied, and pulled one long orange root from the soil. I cleaned it and she merrily chomped away on it, filling herself with the sweet fresh produce. It must have excited her taste buds for it was soon gone and she asked for another.

Picking redcurrants

She spotted the various fruit bushes and quickly sampled gooseberries, raspberries and redcurrants. All these treats seemed to fuel her desire to try yet more of these wonderful flavours.

After an hour of questions her young mind was full of new gardening knowledge, which she soaked up like a sponge, absorbing all the delights of the allotment. I do hope this experience has not only tickled her taste buds but will also give her the ambition in later life to continue discovering the pleasures of gardening and growing your own produce.

It surprises me that some councils are putting pressure on tenants of allotments to use their plots solely for growing vegetables. This might have been the ethos in the past but many people see allotments these days as places of recreation where families can spend time together. I have no problem with a plot being used by a tenant for whatever they see fit, as long as it is kept tidy and in good order, and is not a nuisance to other plot-holders. The main purpose is to spend leisure time in the open air enjoying yourself.

Everyone's approach is different. Mine, I confess, is to cram the plot full of fruit and vegetables to feed myself and my family, although I could be in trouble if I forgot to leave room for the sweet peas!

One season I received a gift of spaghetti squash and sweet American pie pumpkin seeds, sent all the way from California. I bet they wished they were home again in that hot sun after experiencing life on our Welsh hillside!

They grew well on the plot nonetheless, their long green tentacles spreading in profusion across the ground. Like some large ravenous octopus they seemed to swallow everything in their path – potatoes, sweet peas, even the space in between rows of runner beans. No plant was safe from their sprawl. And before long close examination amongst their dense foliage showed some strange objects growing there, white pebble-like squashes and oval green-striped pumpkins already the perfect shape for Cinderella's coach.

Growing pumpkins again brought back happy memories of summers past. At the start of every new season I kept a lookout for someone who was unable to tend their plot that year, and I would offer to cultivate it for them provided I could grow one of my giant pumpkins there, thus satisfying both parties.

I used to grow one of the Atlantic varieties, a giant type making plants that would cover about 24 feet by 13 feet (8 m by 4 m) of soil, and by this month the plant would have produced just one huge baby. This flourished with a very extravagant lifestyle: it grew in a heavily manured piece of ground, had plenty of very rich organic feed and, to make its life more interesting, was treated to six pints of real ale per day. Wouldn't you be happy with that treatment?

This burgeoning monster would be surrounded by empty barrels from drinking happily as the season progressed, and seemed to increase its girth daily as it supped more ale and basked in the sunshine. By October, just in time for Hallowe'en, it would be over 12 stone (75 kg) in weight, and was then ceremonially cut from the plant before being taken off to a local hospital for the weigh-in. After this it was donated to a local school for a series of fundraising events, earning much needed cash for various school projects.

Alas, the great demand for plots these days and the surge in numbers of people wanting to grow their own produce has meant there is never any empty space on the allotments now, and so my annual tradition is lost. But just seeing all the plots full of tasty growing crops reassures me that was a price well worth paying.

PLOT PROGRESS

You don't have to look far on the allotment this month to see progress: it's everywhere. New crops are still going in, others growing vigorously, and the earliest ones coming to fruition at last.

The runner bean rows are looking splendid throughout the allotments, for example, with masses of flowers festooning their green walls. The only problem now is the shortage of bees to carry out the job of pollinating all these blooms, and some of them are dropping off unfertilized. It has come to something that when I do see a bee busily working away on my rows, I move right away from that area so as not to disturb it in its vital task. There is no way I am going to give it an excuse to move to a neighbouring plot and carry on there. In fact there could be some ingenious practices brought into play to entice the bees to my plot if the shortage continues – there could even be some bee rustling going on.

In recent years I have changed my growing pattern to include climbing French beans in half of my row. These fare better in wet conditions as they are self-fertile and don't need the services of a bee to pollinate the flowers, and they hang on the vine a lot longer without becoming tough and fibrous. They generally have a smaller harvest than runner beans, but nevertheless make a tasty addition to the dinner plate, while the surpluses freeze well; little of the flavour is lost, whereas runner beans do lose a little of their freshly picked taste when frozen.

Still, whatever the type of bean, the harvest is in full swing and the favourite crop on the allotments is bringing a smile to all the gardeners there. There is not one plot on the whole site that does not grow this space-saving, productive crop.

Mixed potatoes

There was an unexpected problem with my potato crop one July. With the earlies dug up and cleared, it was time to move on to my second earlies. I grow 'Kestrel', which has a lovely bright purple eye, but on starting to lift these I was disappointed by their small size. On closer examination I noticed these undersized tubers had pink eyes, meaning they were in fact my maincrop variety 'Cara', which should not be ready for weeks yet. I had obviously muddled them up at planting time, and my 'Kestrel' had been planted like a maincrop a fortnight later than required.

It is a strange fact that in the potato world all the different varieties each have their own growth cycle, which is fairly rigidly adhered to regardless of the date when they are planted. So my current crop was a little smaller than hoped for, and I had to wait another two weeks for them to reach full size. Fortunately I love small potatoes with my dinners. Gardening and fresh food might have a healthy effect on the bodies of ageing gardeners, but that does not stop our brain cells playing tricks on us sometimes.

Carrot thinnings

This month there is an extra addition to my food supply, more as a by-product than a crop. The maincrop carrots are growing well, safe from the dreaded root fly within their cage of Enviromesh, and are large enough now for me to harvest a few here and there as thinnings, providing me with tender baby carrots while leaving more room for the rest to grow into those large orange beauties that keep me through the winter.

IN THE GREENHOUSE

Good years . . .

Everything should be growing flat out now, which means that I have to keep up a regular feeding regime to fuel all this vigorous growth, not just outside but under glass too. Tomatoes laden with fruit require almost daily feeding to keep them cropping, for example. Sometimes I am lucky enough to be given a bag of weathered soot, and all I need then is to fill a plastic dustbin with water and steep the soot in a hessian bag to make 'soot water', a traditional rich feed that gives my tomatoes a new dimension to their diet.

Aubergines grow almost as fast as tomatoes in a warm sunny summer, and I start to get excited when I see the plants beginning to throw a lot of pretty light purple flowers, with the promise of some small fruits forming soon. This is still an unusual crop on the Walton menu, so I always keep my fingers crossed that I will have a successful year, so my wife does not have to purchase any to make our own moussaka. That is what I call a triumph!

The only occasional sowing under glass is the regular batches of salad crops in buckets and compartmental trays to fill up the plot, and I can turn part of the greenhouse over to helping me with the harvesting that absorbs more of my energies now. Garlic, for example, has put in a long shift and is showing signs that its growing days are at an end. When the green tops go yellow

Aubergine in flower

Tomatoes are good for you!

There is plenty of evidence about the health benefits of consuming all kinds of fresh fruit and vegetables, and recently the humble tomato was singled out for great praise. A new variety has been bred that contains a high level of selenium, a vital trace element that apparently has good antioxidant properties and helps clean up some of the nasties circulating in our bodies. Most vegetables eaten fresh and grown in safe, clean environments have a positive effect on our health. Now, if green tomatoes could be proved to be a great health booster, I'd be on to a winner, especially in a not so good season!

and the bulbs have swollen to a decent size, they are lifted for drying. The best way to do this is in the sun, but the Welsh climate being what it is (usually wet!) I might have to arrange wire mesh on the greenhouse staging to help them dry thoroughly for winter use.

Shallot tops too are yellowing off, a sure sign they are ready for harvesting. They are lifted from the soil with a fork and the excess soil removed from their roots before they come into the greenhouse with the garlic to finish ripening. Once they are dry with papery skins, I sort out the larger bulbs, which are useful for enhancing my hot dinners, leaving the medium and small ones to land up in jars of spicy vinegar for those winter ploughman's lunches.

. . . and not so good

When July brings cooler, cloudier conditions my large trusses of tomatoes can hang green for weeks on end. Despite feeds high in potash they refuse to ripen into red juicy crops until the sun shines and raises temperatures somewhat. It seems a pity when the plot is producing lots of lettuce, radishes, spring onions and beetroot, yet I still must spend money to finish off the salad bowl with a plump tasteless tomato from the supermarket. Even my cucumbers, which like hot steamy conditions, can overcome dull weather and be laden with fruits while the tomatoes insist on sulking.

When the first tomato does condescend to turn red I assist the ripening process by taking a few bananas that have gone soft with blackening skins and drape these over the lower tomato trusses. According to the chemists the ethylene gas given out by the bananas speeds up ripening and colouring. Granny knew this already when she used to spread out green tomatoes in a drawer with a ripe cut apple, of course.

Bananas used to ripen tomatoes

JULY TASKS

Crops coming to an end

I have been enjoying my rhubarb for several months, with all those tarts and crumbles and my larder filled with various rhubarb jams, and it has served me well. But it's the last days of the harvest now, not because the crop has ceased coming but because it is time to let the plants grow and add vigour back into the crowns before they are exhausted. Also the stalks get richer in oxalic acid as the season progresses, and for those sufferers of gout this can cause a painful reaction. So give it a break – there are plenty of other fruits around now to meet any dessert needs.

Broad beans have finished, too, after filling countless dinner plates and plastic freezer bags, and this has made some good ground available for members of the brassica family. The roots of the broad bean are covered in little nodules which are rich in nitrogen, so I never dig them up. Instead I cut the plants down to ground level and compost the stems – these make rich compostable material and their bulk helps aerate the heap. The roots I leave in place and just clean between the stumps before planting young cabbages in these spaces. This gives the cabbages a head start in life with a nitrogen 'fix', a good way to get a second crop from the same patch for very little effort.

The first early potatoes are also up and eaten, so again there is some very good fertile soil available for seed sowing. Turn this ground over and very often you are rewarded with a few extra potatoes overlooked on the first dig. When raked down to a fine tilth this soil will then be ideal for sowing beetroot, spring onions, kohlrabi and even a row of late peas.

There is nothing like a greedy allotment-holder to make maximum use of ground to supply the kitchen and get the highest return for the rent paid.

Preparing for more strawberries

The strawberry feast is over on my plot and the nets are now removed so that I can tidy up all the plants, which are growing strong and wild. From amongst this dense foliage come lots of long runners bearing young offspring down their length: these are the next generation of strawberry plants ready to be set out for next year.

   The way I do this is to select a strong parent crown and look for a really large youngster attached to one of its runners. I fill a 3-inch (8 cm) pot with compost, sink it in the ground beneath this new plant and pin the youngster down into the pot with a bent piece of wire. It doesn't take long before it is well rooted in this pot, when it can be severed from its 'mother' to grow on independently as a decent young plant for the new strawberry bed. All the tired foliage can then be removed from the old plants and their surplus runners cut away. I then clean up and compost the straw that was tucked under these plants to keep the fruit clean and avoid mildew, and lightly fork over the bed so that it is in good shape for next year.

I replace my strawberry bed every three years to ensure that the health and vigour of the plants does not dwindle and consequently reduce their wonderful succulent crop. With all these free new plants available every year this rotation and annual clean-up is no hardship for a thrifty gardener.

Strawberry runners

Blitzing those slugs

Oh, it can be so hard striving to be totally organic! Replenishing and maintaining the nutrients in my soil using natural materials rather than chemical fertilizers is the easy bit, but when pests are running rampant it can sometimes be hard to resist the temptation to use insecticides for a quick victory.

Patience and persistence usually pay off, however, and the benefits of not using chemicals are worth striving for, but the ever-onward march of slugs and snails is really difficult to accept. The few holes that might appear in the outside leaves of mature crops of brassicas or lettuce come with the territory, but rows of small seedlings disappearing overnight are another matter altogether.

For two years now I have been using nematodes, natural predators applied to the soil to disable and kill the pests, and my slug population seems to be more under control. At this time of year my plot is full of dense foliage, which shelters a thriving group of young frogs that hop around and certainly help the cause, as does the resident family of blackbirds. All I need now is a group of hedgehogs to carry out the night patrol and I might have cracked the problem!

Tanning onions

Most crops might be yielding well, but at this time of year I have no onions, so now is the time when I start harvesting some of my new crop. Yes, they still have green leaves and the bulbs have not reached optimum size, but they are ready for use. Why buy when I have these growing vegetables at my disposal? Sometimes it is necessary to take these actions to achieve my goal of never buying veg again. I just pull what I need for immediate use, leaving the rest to continue to grow in size for drying and storing at summer's end.

By midsummer the crop has plenty of lush green leaves, which the plants need to help swell their bulbs: the more leaves a plant has, the bigger its bulb at harvest time. It is also very important to keep the bed clear of weeds as onions don't like to compete for their food, and they need all they can get to produce top-size bulbs. Another reason a weed-free environment is vital now at the start of the ripening period is that the bulbs must see the sun that turns their skin golden brown. Even onions enjoy a good suntan!

Growing my greens

When at the end of the three years the strawberry plants are cleared, the bed is turned over to make a new home for my winter greens. Space is always at a premium this time of year and this new piece of empty ground is a saviour for those crops that need a long growing season. I usually plant six each of many varieties of savoy cabbage, purple sprouting broccoli and winter cabbage.

The bed is raked over, with a sprinkling of blood, fish and bone and concentrated manure dug well in to give plants a lift when they are settled in. Then I spread a light covering of lime to sweeten the soil – brassicas don't like acid conditions. Each plant is popped into a hole lined with lime and filled with fresh multi-purpose compost to reduce the risk of club root disease. Although these crops are for winter and next spring, it's important not to forget to put protective collars around their stems to stop any attack from cabbage root fly, which is still on the wing.

For several years I did not bother much with spring cabbages, which on our hillside are always a target for wood pigeons looking for a feast in the dark days of winter, but that left a gap in my supply of greens to the table. As I am now the owner of some good bird netting and some strong frames, protection is at hand and so I started growing spring cabbage again.

I was surprised to find that 'Flower of Spring' and 'Wheeler's Imperial', which I remember from years back, are still the varieties most widely grown. I like to sow a half-size seed tray of each, and when the seedlings are large enough they are pricked out into twelve-cell compartmental trays, making enough plants to fill that annoying interval in the greens supply far ahead next spring. In doing this I am returning to my roots, because these always used to be my first cabbages of the year.

Cabbages protected with net

Food rationing

Whereas my onions and winter vegetables are fed at least twice weekly throughout July to ensure they make big strong growth, the end of the month for me is the time to end my feeding regime. I stop being generous after this month so that the plants are encouraged to channel all the goodness in their foliage back into the roots. I don't want too much soft green growth as we head into autumn, and with July ticking on it is time to encourage tough hardy plants with good harvest potential.

This applies particularly to onions, fed regularly on sheep manure steeped in water to bolster their size. Now it is more important for the plants to concentrate on storing food in those swelling bulbs, hardening them up for keeping through to next spring. The same goes for leeks as I don't want too much soft foliage on them that might suffer in the cold days of winter. Runner and French beans on the other hand are very greedy and I need to keep them flourishing and cropping well, so they continue to be served their lavish diet of wormery water and seaweed extract three times a week.

Keeping on top of sweet peas

The whole plot has an air of beauty and fragrance about it now that my large hedge of sweet peas is in full flower. These scented blooms need regular feeding and almost daily cutting while they are in peak condition, so it is not only the Walton household that boasts large vases of them everywhere. Many of my gardening buddies benefit from this plentiful supply too, just another example of the constant sharing that makes gardening such a friendly pastime.

Looking back

It is amazing how the writers of that popular TV sit-com *The Good Life* could have foreseen way back in the 1970s the reality as it is now in the second decade of the twenty-first century.

Apparently many more people are giving over part of their gardens to growing fruit and vegetables, and (unlike in the TV series) there is no outcry from neighbours about this silent revolution. Continual inflation of the price of food is driving this change to the basic grow-your-own culture: the days of cheap food are no more, and are unlikely to return. So lawns are disappearing and herbaceous borders shrinking as the momentum towards providing at least some of your own food continues to grow.

The final step to serious self-sufficiency is still to become widely taken, and pigs or cows are not yet in the ascendancy in urban back gardens. But it is only a matter of time. Already there is a steady return to the old practice of keeping a few laying hens – witness the increased sales of the very plush, moveable hen houses now available. Just half a dozen hens can provide a daily supply of fresh eggs, while the birds will help to keep down slugs, eat all those vegetable off-cuts, and give you manure to enrich your veg patch as a bonus. As many of us found just a generation ago, in fact.

Meanwhile seed companies are gleefully noting a rapid and steady increase in sales of vegetable seeds compared with flowers, and the industry is currently worth over £60 million per year. All that needs to be done now is to reinstate those 50,000 or more allotments that have been taken from us in recent decades.

Up the gardening revolution, I say!

JULY IN A NUTSHELL

Key jobs for JULY

- Pick soft fruits as they ripen before the birds beat you to them.
- Harvest and freeze some early runner beans while at their best.
- Thin maincrop carrots and use the tender thinnings for the dinner plate.
- Feed greenhouse crops regularly with various fertilizers.
- Harvest autumn-sown garlic.
- Harvest shallots.

If you have time . . .

- Clean up strawberry beds, removing old leaves and weeds from them.

Looking ahead to AUGUST

- Keep netting winter brassicas to ward off cabbage white butterflies.
- Stock up the freezer with surplus crops.
- Harvest onions when dry and string up in a cool dry place.
- Harvest courgettes regularly before they become large marrows.
- Prepare composting areas with all the green waste coming off the plot.

Picking gooseberries

Thought for the month

Despite everything that might be thrown at us to challenge us during the gardening year, a gardener is a happy soul and tends to cope admirably with these variable elements. We enjoy our hobby, and that is half our secret.

So it always saddens me to read yet another article about the trend towards hard-landscaped and low-maintenance gardens. To me there is no such thing as truly low-maintenance gardening: even all that decking and paving needs regular cleaning. Shrubs might be small when bought, but quickly grow and overflow their allotted patch of ground, and then have to be pruned back hard or replaced altogether to keep the garden in perspective.

To a seasoned gardener like myself, and many others on allotments everywhere, there is nothing more therapeutic than pulling out a few weeds and constantly harvesting or replacing plants. This brings variety to the gardener's everyday life, and they do say variety is the spice of life. A constantly growing and evolving garden is a treat to behold every day, and walking round observing these changes lifts and invigorates me. If you don't believe me, try it!

AUGUST

HERE WE ARE, KNOCKING ON THE DOOR of late summer. August is a month of bountiful harvests and the time to enjoy to the full the huge selection of vegetables and fruits that are at their zenith of perfection.

Summer may continue to tease but usually we can look forward to some very warm days this month, even though the nights are cooler and we may already be feeling the breath of autumn.

This is a relaxed time on the plot, now the spate of planting and sowing has slowed to a trickle and our endeavours are being rewarded. The routine changes significantly and daily tasks become fewer. Just attack a few weeds with your trusty hoe, leave them to shrivel in the midday sun, and don't fret about those bare patches of soil that are gradually becoming visible here and there. Like the gardener, the plot deserves its period of rest too after giving of its best.

My sweet peas seem to have produced a million blooms all summer, but by now are increasingly difficult to harvest, as any remaining blossoms are way above my head. Their stems are becoming much shorter but I can still cut a nice posy to add colour and fragrance to our home. Experts say the plants should be layered by cutting free each stem from its cane, trailing it along the ground and then training it up another cane to carry on with the flowering season, but this seems like 'mission impossible' on my dense hedge, and I am afraid that my peace offering whenever I arrive home late from the allotments will soon cease. Still, there are my chrysanthemums growing in the background, and within the next few weeks these will become my saviour.

Too many courgettes

August is a golden, more relaxed month on the allotment, filled with pleasurable hours of gathering harvests, the reward for all that early preparation and work.

The problem is that some crops mature faster than I can eat the produce. One in particular is the courgette – as many people find, once they start yielding, the plants seem unstoppable. The fruits will keep for quite a while in a cool place, but there are only so many anyone can eat fresh.

That is why this time of year will often find me in the kitchen making preserves that can be used in the long winters to spice up cold meat dishes. Courgettes are the perfect vegetable to make into chutneys – boiled with onions, mixed spice, apple, malt vinegar, fresh ginger and brown sugar, they make the perfect relish. And there will still be many left over for a ratatouille or two.

Stay vigilant

During late summer many garden pests are planning their survival tactics for the long winter ahead, and are urgently seeking out the young tender parts of plants to gorge on.

Those pretty cabbage white butterflies still fill the air in abundance as they seek out your winter brassicas on which to deposit clutches of eggs. This late batch of caterpillars will soon munch its way through your Brussels sprouts before clambering off to dry places in your sheds and under overhangs to pupate over winter.

Aphids are multiplying at an enormous rate, following the principle that the more of them there are the more will survive winter. The carrot root fly is also on the lookout for late carrots where it can raise its young to ensure that the pest will return to plague us again next season.

Go on, use all the weapons in your armoury to combat these pests – my finger-and-thumb technique will be working overtime, crushing these blighters. The high-pressure sprayer will be in use daily, washing colonies off plants and halting their multiplication. Vigilance is the key to controlling all these garden pests because, have no fear, they will be back.

Ripeness is all

Any sunshine we get this month is just what we need to help ripen crops for autumn harvest. My onions, for example, are beginning to lower their leaves, a sure sign that their growing cycle is coming to an end. This action exposes their white swollen bulbs to the sun, giving them the last chance to put on weight before acquiring their bright rich tan colour.

When this ripening stage is over, they can be carefully lifted, to complete the drying process in a cool, airy greenhouse. Then I string them up in plaited ropes, making it easy to pluck one from its bunch whenever an onion is needed for a tasty dish.

The approach of autumn

As late August draws near, the allotments lose their youthful appearance and begin to age. The rows of beans show tinges of yellow on their leaves, even though they continue to give a good harvest. I try, with a feed of seaweed extract, to stimulate them into extending their cropping season a little longer.

But it is not only the plot that is beginning to exhibit those shades of autumn's golds and russets: the mountain bracken is turning brown by the end of this month, and the surrounding trees are acquiring their autumn tints. The allotments and their surroundings are all starting to look tired after another great season of growth and harvest.

Tales from the plot

One vegetable that suffers in the almost daily rainfall of recent summers is the maincrop potato. The tall leggy haulm cannot withstand too much wetting when the weather is humid, and tends to fall victim to its dreaded enemy, potato blight. Then it is a race against time to dig up the crop before the blight spores are washed down to the tubers, causing them to rot. Everyone on the plots is doing the same.

As the proud possessor of a large supply of paper sacks, courtesy of my local pet store, I seem to have acquired a new role in this salvage operation. Roger and Carl, who always have bumper crops of potatoes, promptly beat a path to my shed to scrounge some of these sacks, which depletes my paper mountain but at least releases a little more space in my cluttered shed.

I always look forward to turning over the empty patch once my potato crop is lifted, for below the surface lurk the tubers that escaped my clutches first time round. I consider these a bonus gift, a little like 'road kill', and it is surprising how many of these hidden tubers I discover despite my best harvesting endeavours.

I have a short drive from my home to the allotment (yes, it is a little too far to walk these days), and on my way I usually think about the jobs for the morning so that I am organized and ready to get on with them on my arrival.

However, the other week Ron had found a source of 'black gold' – a gardener's term for very old, well-rotted manure – and had managed to borrow Dai's flat-back lorry. So an intrepid band of Brian, myself and Ron at the wheel set off to collect this essential material, complete with a pile of empty plastic bags on the back bed.

When we arrived at this secret destination we were able to park right alongside a whole mountain of this good stuff. It looked fabulous to us, although only a gardener would regard horse manure with that much affection. We set to work filling all the bags and in due course were on our way back to the allotments, gloating over our bounty on board.

On our return Albie was at the ready with cups of coffee while we distributed the bags equally amongst the group. Cooperation and teamwork is part of the culture of being an allotmenteer, proving that the old adage 'many hands make light work' still holds up.

But my careful plans for that morning were well and truly scuppered.

It is bragging time now as plot-holders vie for 'Best on Site', and there is plenty of to-ing and fro-ing as you are requested to 'Have a look at my onions' or 'Just look at the length of these beans'. This is when the allotment wags come to the fore, and there is usually a cry from behind a bean row of 'Help, will someone come and give me a hand to lift this cabbage!'

Carl and Terry S are masters of the art of wind-up, which makes for good spirit and banter across the plots. Despite this, though, there is always a willingness to help out those whose crops have failed. Poor old Fred, for example, has had no success with his beans, and he has taken a lot of stick. We were sitting on our usual bench last week for the morning coffee when Fred joined us, complaining about his poor crop and a bit put out by the harvests that we all seemed to be gathering.

'It's my first year,' he said, 'so I bought this gardening book and worked to that.'

'Well, don't lend it to me, Fred,' I said. 'It's local knowledge, not books, that produces the crops.'

But he went home with a bagful of beans donated from all sources.

One August morning a stranger arrived at the allotment bearing a special gift for me. It was Richard from the company Wiggly Wigglers, with numerous parcels containing my very own wormery, a composting heaven.

He set about constructing it. First he put the feet on the large reservoir at the bottom where, he told me, the super-rich 'worm wee' collected. At this stage it looked more like a barbecue than anything that might produce compost. Next came the real action chamber, the home for the worms. These normally live in some soaked coir compost, but in my case I had some superb Welsh home-made compost to give these worms a flying start in their new home.

Then Richard opened the bag containing a writhing mass of special worms that were going to begin work for me. He said there were a thousand of them now under my control, although I was not going to count them. In they went into the compost and were duly covered with a special mat to keep them warm and happy.

The most vital instruction for their future well-being was to add small but regular supplies of kitchen waste, on which they feed. Beware, though! They are fussy eaters and don't like citrus fruit or onion parts. All other kitchen waste (no meat, mind you) is gratefully received, even tea bags, kitchen roll and tissues. Further material is only added when the majority of the previous waste has been consumed.

A few weeks after acquiring the wormery I already had a plentiful supply of juices on which to feed my plants, plus a chamber on level one full of well-munched compost. Level two was added then, and the worms migrated into the next storey of their dwelling. Only the penthouse chamber was left to add, at which point I could start using compost from the base chamber for my plants.

Now we have a ceramic jar permanently stationed in the corner of our kitchen where all the waste is collected. The only moan my wife has is that it must be cut up small before adding to the jar – oh, how we spoil these worms, but they deserve it!

I am often asked what is special about being an organic gardener. Well, mastering the art depends on building a natural ecosystem and encouraging wildlife to be an integral part of the gardening regime.

Nature usually has a simple solution, which you just need to find to unlock the door to the benefits of this increasingly popular way of life. Part of the secret lies in improving the soil with plenty of organic matter: build up its fertility and the good health of your plants will be able to ward off many of the pests and diseases nature throws at them. Rotation is also a major factor in boosting a crop's resistance, helping reduce the number of pests and diseases.

Every pest has a predator of some kind, and you just have to encourage those predators to take up residence in your garden. Attract them by planting the flowers and plants they love and they will soon colonize your patch, feeding copiously on those pests that may visit. Use other natural forms of pest control (insecticides kill friend as well as foe), such as spraying with clean fresh water or constant use of finger and thumb to nip infestations in the bud.

Vigilance is key! Regular inspection and careful management of the garden is essential, while spotting early signs of problems allows you to deal with issues before they overwhelm plants. Above all enjoy your garden, try to be kind to all that lives there, and enjoy the harvests that your new gardening regime brings.

Salad days are well and truly back! What is more pleasant than to sit on your patio of a beautiful evening and enjoy a plate of lettuce, tomatoes and cucumber, interspersed with the slightly burning taste of radish and the tang of an onion, all gathered fresh from the plot only hours earlier? Just a glass of white wine in hand, and all is again right with the world.

Harvest home

A flood of produce has shifted the workload from my hillside plot to my kitchen as the time arrives to stock the store for the long days ahead.

The shallots have been graded, with the smaller ones finding a winter home in jars of spiced vinegar. The garlic crop has been lifted too and has produced some super bulbs after all the rain. The individual cloves within are plump and taste fabulous eaten soon after harvesting. Most of the bulbs, however, are spread out in the sunshine to ripen fully, ready for storing to reward me all winter.

With onions swelling in girth, some have been harvested in the quest to make use of the inevitable surfeit of courgettes. Cooked with brown sugar and vinegar, the two vegetables have been transformed into jars of tasty, tangy chutney to accompany my cold meat dishes with wonderful flavours and memories of summer in the months ahead. All I

Crop of courgettes

Picking peas

need now is some sunshine to hasten the ripening of my tomatoes and peppers, and then life in the 'soup kitchen' will begin.

The last pickings of blackcurrants and gooseberries are no longer needed for tarts but have been made into wonderful jam, and the larder is filling up with those lovely jars that look so pristine with their bright labels describing the wonderful contents hidden within.

Surplus runner beans and French beans have been sliced and bagged, and are starting to fill those empty spaces in my freezer. The peas produced a very heavy yield, and they have been podded within hours of harvesting to freeze in all that tasty summer goodness, ready to be released again during the long dark winter months.

If the harvests continue at this rate there will be a need for me to spend money on another chest freezer, but it has not come to that drastic stage . . . yet.

Pumpkin guard duty

Despite the continual battering it took from all the summer rain and wind, my prize large pumpkin finally produced an offspring. Although the plant did not look its healthiest best, nevertheless it did its job and by August there was a tennis-ball-size fruit on the main stem. It needed lifting carefully on to a square of heavy duty plastic to keep it up from the sodden soil and prevent it from rotting.

With masses of sideshoots and regular feeding supporting the plant's efforts to produce a great yellow ball of sunshine, I could leave it to the task of swelling the little beauty while I turned my attention to guarding it

The pumpkin patch

religiously from preying slugs and snails for the next few weeks. Curbing the appetite of these hungry molluscs involves a nightly patrol by torchlight, clothed in black and face covered up, with old kitchen knife in hand. As Corporal Jones in *Dad's Army* would say, 'They don't like it up them.' This is a sure-fire way of protecting plants, and totally organic too.

Company under glass

While busy in my greenhouse the other day I noticed a couple of bees popping in with little pieces of leaf. There are a few pots around with dry compost still in them, and the bees were stuffing the leaf fragments into holes they must each have dug out earlier. These were leaf-cutting bees preparing their nests, using the bits of leaf to build cells in which the eggs are laid and the larvae develop. I always think of bees as social insects living in hives, but there are many species of these useful pollinators that lead solitary lives, far more than I thought. The garden is a wonderful place to learn some of the secrets of nature.

Not all insects have the same warm relationship with gardeners, though, and as the season progresses the wasp stops being useful and can become a nuisance while we try to enjoy the great outdoors. Unlike the bee, which is loath to sting and then only in self-defence, the wasp is an aggressive creature and seems to terrorize for fun. In the early part of the season wasps perform valuable work in the garden, chasing down garden pests to feed their young. But once these adolescents leave the nest, the workers' task is done and they start making our lives a misery.

So remember, don't eat or drink anything sugary in the open air in August or you'll be an immediate target. This is nature in the raw, and we have to take the good along with the bad.

IN THE GREENHOUSE

Mixed fortunes

Away from the vagaries of the weird summer weather we have experienced recently, life in the greenhouse continues at its normal pace, safe from the cold and wet outside. My tomatoes are yielding plenty of large red fruits, essential for so many dishes, and what a joy it is to pick them: once enough are steadily ripening, there is the added satisfaction of being able to pop the occasional one into my mouth to sustain me during my gardening chores.

Cucumbers tend to do well whatever the weather, and by now are throwing lots of long green fruits – many more than I can consume, so friends and family share in these bumper crops. The vines have reached the top of the greenhouse where they can trail at will and hang in great profusion from the wires and canes in the roof. I love August with all this super produce!

Glut of cucumbers

A male flower on a melon

The first fruits have shown on my aubergines and have set so well that all bodes fair for a crop later in the summer. The plants are full of purple flowers now, and I shall have to watch carefully and remove some so as not to overburden the plants with trying to bring too many fruits to maturity.

Only the melon still limps along in a cool year, sometimes not even reaching staging height where it can roam free. There are many male flowers on it – they always appear first – but no visible sign yet of a female. The challenge is on, and I urgently want the weather to improve if I am to harvest one of these luscious tropical fruits.

AUGUST TASKS

Holiday plans

This is a time of year when some allotmenteers slide away for a holiday with their families. The allotment is always a great place to be, but a break from those daily excursions sometimes recharges the batteries, and it is a great relief if you know that you can leave your precious plants in the hands of someone who has nearly the same affection for them as yourself. The watering will be done and any ripe crops will be harvested in your absence.

However, before you go make sure you have gathered in all those vegetables that do not want to remain on the plant for any length of time. Runner beans, French beans and courgettes all need picking regularly to keep those harvests coming, so take home everything that is ready before you go, and tell the neighbouring plot-holder who is looking after the plot for you to keep picking and to take the produce by way of thanks. Freeze the beans you have gathered, and store the courgettes in a cool place such as the shed (they will keep perfectly fresh while you're away).

All the red tomatoes in the greenhouse need gathering (these freeze well); then whatever cucumbers and tomatoes ripen in your absence can go to your kind 'babysitter'.

The last job to do before your break is to give everything a feed of liquid fertilizer to sustain it in your absence. Then go away with peace of mind, knowing all is in good hands.

Filling the gaps

As harvesting progresses this month gaps begin to appear along my plot. Although it is nearing that time of year when the shortening daylight hours signal that sowing time is coming to an end, this ground cannot be left empty just yet and I cannot resist the challenge to use it productively.

Salad features high on the eating regime in the Walton household, and a few fast-maturing crops of radishes, lettuce and beetroot will fill these spaces. Then, if the rest of the summer is kind, salads for my table should continue for many weeks yet.

Two weeks ago I sowed some 'Valdor' lettuces in pots and they have already grown into stout little plants. I am going to plant them out a little earlier than I normally would so that they can get established in these shorter days. This will allow me time to make yet another sowing of these hardy autumn lettuces and give them a taste of fresh air before they are cosseted under a cloche to provide me with lettuce throughout the autumn months.

'Valdor' lettuce

Gambling with beans

My second early potatoes need lifting since their tops are disappearing fast, a signal they are ready. After digging they are left on the surface of the soil overnight to partially dry, and then I stack them in plastic trays in my shed to complete the drying process, making sure they are covered to exclude light or they will turn green and poisonous. Once they are dry I remove any damaged ones before storing the rest in paper sacks, which keep them dark and absorb any remaining moisture.

The ground vacated will be called straight back into action to accommodate my experimental broad beans, sown late to see if I can get an autumn crop. They have made rapid progress in their little polystyrene cups, surprising me by the speed of their growth, and they are ready to go out now. A top dressing of blood, fish and bone will boost the still fertile soil and give them a flying start. It will be interesting to find out if these mature before winter and provide an extra crop to fill the freezer.

Sweeter corn

By now one of my favourite end-of-season crops stands over 6 feet (1.8 m) tall – yes, my sweetcorn is looking very promising. I have already started to harvest the 'mini-pops', small immature cobs which are perfect for stirfries and salads, but it is the big, yellow, full-size cobs that I am impatient for.

This crop enjoys the late summer warmth and we have plenty of regular rainfall here in Wales to keep it growing skywards, so the cobs are already filling out nicely. The advantage of growing your own sweetcorn is that the cobs can be cooked very soon after being harvested, maintaining the delicate balance of sweetness – the longer they are left, the more sugar turns to starch and perfection is lost.

It is time to check if they are ready by peeling back the outer sheath of a cob to see if the kernels are yellow. If so, squeeze a kernel with your

Sweetcorn

thumbnail, and if it oozes a white milky fluid it is ready. I choose as many cobs as I am going to eat immediately, harvest them in their green leafy covering, and on arrival home pop them straight in the microwave for four minutes. Take them out, leave to stand for two minutes, then strip off the leaves, roll the cob in butter, and savour that heavenly taste!

Completing the circle

As the many harvests are collected in, so the spent green waste grows in volume, providing yet more material to compost, to form next year's soil conditioner.

As I did with the weeds earlier in the growing season (see page 143), I need to mix this green waste with plenty of well-rotted manure, so it is off to my local stables – at this time of year the stuff is lighter to carry and far easier to shift than when laden with water. The compost heap is built with interleaved layers of green waste and horse manure, adding to each layer my secret ingredient (pigeon manure), which is rich in nitrogen and

Simple mould control

The whole family of cucurbits – cucumbers, courgettes, marrows and pumpkins – need to be watched carefully during August as any warm humid nights will create ideal conditions for the onset of mildew. This white patchy growth on the foliage can be discouraged easily by cutting off any older leaves that are affected and discarding them. Then a light spray all over and under the remaining leaves with one part milk and ten parts water will help control a fresh mildew outbreak. The fungus needs acid conditions to thrive, and the milky water, being alkaline, will restrict it.

Mildew on courgette plant

helps stoke up the heat that produces good friable compost. To retain the heat, I cover the heap with a large black plastic sheet, which also absorbs extra heat from outside when the sun shines.

Next spring, the sheet is removed and the fabulous contents of the heap will be ready to add to the plot to increase its fertility and yield strong, healthy crops. In the organic gardening world soil condition is the key to success, and this organic matter encourages earthworms, which aerate the soil, and boosts the micro-organisms that help plant roots thrive.

So all the waste from the plot is returned in this new form to enliven the soil and produce a great growing medium. The circle of life is complete.

Looking back

One great favourite on the old-fashioned plot was a clump of mint for making savoury mint sauce. Many of the folk in the neighbouring houses used to stroll into the allotments on a Sunday morning to beg a fresh bunch to add that relish to the Sunday lunch, but the custom died out. So it was a surprise the other Sunday when someone actually came in and asked for some. Maybe the old days are returning to this Welsh valley!

And it is not just human visitors we occasionally see on our allotment site. During my years here we have had quite a few alien creatures found among the crops: rabbits, toads, even the odd fox. The local cats are regularly to be seen roaming the paths looking for a mouse or two. Sadly, though, for some long while there has been no sign of a hedgehog – sorely missed as an ally in the crusade to suppress all our slugs.

The other evening I was surprised to receive a phone call from Ron saying, 'You'll never guess what I have just found on my plot.' It was a terrapin, something we had never seen there before. It was not much practical use in gardening terms, so it was duly removed and settled into a new home with the son of one of our members. Clearly one is never alone on an allotment!

AUGUST IN A NUTSHELL

Key jobs for AUGUST

✔ Use surplus produce to make chutneys and jams.

✔ Ripen onions to ensure they keep well.

✔ Dry second early potatoes thoroughly after lifting before storing in paper sacks.

✔ Make sure plot is weeded and well fed before embarking on a well-earned holiday.

✔ Check if sweetcorn is ripe and ready to harvest.

✔ Prepare a compost-heap area for all that surplus material coming off the plot.

If you have time . . .

✔ Bring your rotation plan up to date as crops finish or are moved.

Looking ahead to SEPTEMBER

✔ Start to remove climbing beans from their supports and compost this bulky material.

✔ Mark out plot according to your crop rotation plan ready to prepare areas to suit their new inhabitants.

✔ Prune soft-fruit bushes.

✔ Stake Brussels sprouts to stop winter weather loosening their roots.

✔ Collect those falling leaves to make fabulous leafmould.

✔ Order sets of garlic and autumn onions for autumn planting.

Courgette harvest

Thought for the month

The allotment food boom goes on and on this month, and I know I have reached the peak of the cropping season when my wife utters the words, 'What am I going to do with all these vegetables?'

But use them we do: our daily diet is very healthy and we are living almost a vegetarian existence at this time of the year. The freezer never seems big enough, as copious amounts of runner and French beans go in to join the broad beans and peas. Judging by the number of bags, boxes and other containers members are carrying out of the allotment gates, they are all producing similarly bountiful crops – the whole of the Rhondda valley must be feasting on vegetables.

It makes me wonder why this country has to import produce when one allotment site in the centre of the valley can feed so many. If this action were replicated up and down the country many more would become self-sufficient on local produce, and environmental issues would be eased no end. Yet we have seen acres of green land disappear below tarmac and concrete, with the result in many areas that there are insufficient plots to meet the demand and growing waiting lists.

I would urge everyone to go to their local authority and insist on an allotment. It is everyone's statutory right, and if six or more people request one, the authority is legally bound to meet the demand (though within no obligatory timeframe – so the more pressure the better). Come on, councils, provide more plots and help the cause!

SEPTEMBER

NOWHERE IS THE PASSING OF THE YEAR more evident than in the garden. When I am sowing, it is spring; when I am harvesting, it is summer; the autumn is preparation time. And as I am in preparation mode, it must be autumn and the end of the gardening year!

Around September the mix of people working on the allotments starts to change. There are some plot-holders who only grow summer vegetables, and as their patch empties they turn it over and hibernate throughout the winter months. To me they are missing out on the pleasures of fresh vegetables all year round.

I appreciate that many of the winter crops now left on the plot occupy the ground for a long period, and vegetables like parsnips, leeks and sprouts have been growing there for many months, joined in May by swedes which can be started a bit later. But the taste of these winter vegetables brings a change of flavours to the palate.

They also have the advantage in those long barren months ahead of not needing much attention – no watering, no feeding and very little weeding. What more could you ask? If you have not tried growing winter vegetables, give it a go even though your fingers get cold harvesting them and there is the occasional trickle of rainwater down your neck.

There are still many reasons to go down to the plot every day, though, and not just to keep in touch with my allotmenteering friends. My chrysanthemums are in full bloom, shining like colourful beacons. I think my wife cherishes a bunch of these more than the large boxes of vegetables I bring home each day. There is no accounting for taste!

With the growing season drawing to a close, it is possible now to take stock of how crops have performed with regard to the kind of weather we have had.

After a wet, lacklustre summer the crop I find suffering more than most on my hillside is sweetcorn. There might be some big cobs on the plants, but on peeling back their outer leaves for a closer look inside I may well find they are still not yet ready for harvesting. They like hot, dry days, and when these have been in short supply their deep yellow kernels refuse to form, so I have to keep checking. Hope springs eternal that late September may see a flush of warmth to bring these cobs to perfection.

As long as there are no early frosts my autumn raspberries will carry on ripening, and any welcome warmth and sunshine in early September will give them a boost. They are the last of the soft fruits on the plot, their sweet red berries making an excellent filling for meringue nests. When they finally finish providing me with their tasty crop, I cut the fruited branches right back to ground level. This will give them a winter's rest before the new young shoots emerge from the soil next year.

Prepare for surprises!

In the strange twists and turns of one gardening year I was amazed by the amount of new tender stalks that appeared from my rhubarb crowns after I stopped cropping them in midsummer. These were tempting to pull, just to taste again the flavour of a rhubarb crumble. But no, I had my fill of this early 'fruit' and it would benefit the crown if these stalks and leaves were left to send all that extra feed back down into the roots. A fit and healthy crown could then stand forcing for an early crop in March next year. The secret of good gardening is never to be too greedy.

Another surprise is often the courgettes. One wet August these were beginning to turn yellow and were covered with downy mildew. I was going to consign them to the compost heap but, as often happens on the allotment, other jobs took priority. Much to my amazement the plants made some fresh, healthy growth and were giving a second crop of young courgettes in September. With a good stock keeping fresh in the shed, plus plenty of courgette chutney on the shelf, there was a good chance of my wife converting these extra fruits into moist, tasty courgette loaf.

Staying on guard

When will those dreaded cabbage white butterflies ever go away and let me relax? Even now my late cabbages may be attacked despite my rhubarb liquid spray, and so I must resort to covering them with a net. Despite this protection I am sometimes horrified to discover caterpillars nibbling away at the plants under the net – they must manage to sneak through my defences or perhaps crawl there from a nearby plot. They are quickly despatched, though not before they've done some damage to my crop. There is no dropping your guard on an organic plot and a watchful eye is always needed.

Caterpillars on cabbages

Who's the boss?

A sure sign that the food supply for the birds in the surrounding countryside is beginning to diminish is that my neighbourhood robin has taken me back under his wing, so to speak, and seems to be with me everywhere. He is watching and waiting for me to disturb some soil or turn over a few leaves and uncover some tasty morsels to satisfy his appetite. I was forsaken all summer while he raised his brood, but now they have flown the nest he is back – and in territorial mode, fighting off all rivals for my patch of ground. Who is actually in charge on this plot? It certainly isn't me!

Check the leeks

If wet conditions persist throughout late summer, there is always a risk of rust spots appearing on some of my leeks. Provided they have grown well, they should be large plants by now and the rust should have very little effect on them this late in the season. I deal with it by removing affected outer leaves, disposing of these well away from the plot to stop further spread and prevent spores lingering on my plot.

There is apparently a way of controlling the spread of these spores by a physical barrier, and this involves rubbing the affected leaves with a coating of Vaseline, which seals the spores in and stops them being dispersed on to other plants. This sounds reasonable in theory. The trouble is that giving all this meticulous attention to my 105 leek plants is really a step too far for me!

Tales from the plot

Traditions and habits have changed significantly over the years on our hillside allotment. During the 1950s and 60s there was hardly a building to be seen on the very open-plan site, and the only structures were the store sheds where bulk fertilizers were stocked and sold to tenants.

A gradual revolution occurred as plot-holders began to see the added value to life on the plot of first a shed then a greenhouse. It was not long before every plot had one of each – not purchased, I hasten to add (at least where greenhouses were concerned) but put together from recycled materials. My greenhouse went up in the late 1960s, fashioned from one of those prefabricated dwellings that were built during the Second World War to house the bombed-out population. The windows are made of cast aluminium and will last forever, and these are bound together with wooden joists from replaced floors. The roof did cost me a penny or two, it must be said, as I had to purchase corrugated plastic sheets to keep out the rain. This recycled greenhouse has been home over the years to many thousands of plants, and I have a fond attachment to it.

It was a sad day when I began to doubt whether its door, which had been creaking for some time, would survive another winter. Now, 'never buy if you can beg or borrow' is the allotmenteers' motto, and so I spread the word around the allotments that I was looking for a replacement door.

Blow me down: Keith arrived very soon afterwards with his trailer in tow, and nestled in the back was an exact replica of the door that had lasted me more than twenty years. He had been driving down the valley and just happened to spot this door in a skip. The skip raiders had triumphed once more!

September can be wet here on the allotments. 'Black Friday', for example, was a whole day of dark clouds and lashing rain continually falling from a leaden sky. I went on my daily sortie to the plot at mid-morning to harvest a few crops and found the path was already a raging torrent. There was no one else around, so I didn't dally for long.

On Saturday morning, even before I reached the gates, there was strong evidence of what might lie ahead. The street outside was littered with debris of stone and gravel, piled high across the road. Inside there was no sign of our main pathway, and the gates themselves were impossible to open as debris was piled high against them.

After a determined struggle I managed to get in, and the first sight was Albie's café, still intact but cut off by a deep ravine – should we build a bridge to it, or go and collect the path from outside the allotment? Soon plot-holders started to arrive and, wheelbarrows at the ready, restored the path. Then there was the major task of draining a new lake that had formed at the bottom of Terry S's plot. The sloping ground there could hold no more water, and the constant run-off created this new but unwelcome water feature.

With plenty of willing hands we were soon shipshape once more. It's all in a day's work on the plot.

Another Friday there was an unexpected flurry of activity on the allotment as our annual skip arrived. Allotmenteers normally raid skips for buried treasure that can be reused on the allotment, so it was a novel experience to see many of them filling this one with discarded rubbish from their plots.

It had not been there more than a couple of hours when it was full to capacity. I was elsewhere when it was delivered, and it was fortunate that Dai H rang me to inform me it had come, because I had my old greenhouse door to get rid of – now that Keith had come across a replacement. I immediately asked Dai if he would throw it on before the skip was full – and lucky that I did, for by the time I arrived at the allotments it was perilously overloaded with no room whatever for another item.

I was on the phone straight away to have it removed. But disaster struck before the day was over, because the lorry sent to fetch it hit our smart new bench, and now there is an unplanned repair job waiting for Brian on his next visit to the allotments.

Many things change hands in the continual bartering on the allotments, and I thought I had witnessed every possible kind of exchange for surplus crops, but it seems there are still surprises to be found here even after fifty years.

The other week Bolts came walking down Brian's path carrying a large handful of beans. Several minutes later Bolts was walking up Brian's path carrying a small bag. Then all went quiet as they both entered his shed.

Curiosity got the better of Albie and me, so we went to investigate and found Brian sitting there comfortably while Bolts was cutting his hair. Clearly the latest exchange rate for a handful of beans is a haircut. I wonder if beans could become an international currency and replace the troubled euro!

One day I ventured to the far side of the allotments – a trip I don't have time to do during the summer – to see what those 'people on the hill' were up to. On my way back I stopped suddenly, my attention distracted by the aroma of fresh coffee. Not being one to ignore such an enticing and unusual smell, I followed my nose, which led me to Bob's shed. There, sitting comfortably in his armchair, was Bob himself enjoying his aromatic brew. The look on my face must have spoken volumes because within minutes Bob had poured me a mugful, and offered a comfortable chair where I could sit and savour it at my leisure.

Beware, Albie: there is an upmarket establishment in the neighbourhood that could be vying for my custom in the future!

In this era of hosepipe bans, water shortages and metering, collecting rainwater makes good sense – it falls freely (very freely in Wales!) from the sky and collecting it fits the allotment philosophy of thrift.

Recently I acquired two new water butts to add to my already sizeable collection. Mine are filled from my shed and greenhouse roofs, and they are fitted with pipes that duct surplus water to overflow butts. Rainwater is better for plants than mains water, as it contains no fluorides or chlorides, and only natural elements are present. I find too that watering from a barrel which has been standing in the sun gives plants a warm soak rather the chill of water from a hosepipe. Soon it will be time to empty these butts, clean them out and then let them refill, ready for next year's drought.

I have a habit of placing my mobile phone in my shirt pocket, and it is forever falling out when I am on the plot. Usually I hear it go and can find it, but the other week, after doing several different tasks, I went to my pocket and found the phone gone. Despite frantically revisiting all the places where I thought I had been, there was no sign of it.

Of course, just when you need them there was nobody on the allotment. I had to go over to Albie's house to borrow his mobile and ring my number. After a few minutes' searching I could just hear a faint ringing from my Brussels sprouts, and there it was, tucked out of sight in among the huge leaves. I will have to check my bill when it arrives in case some crafty slug made a sneaky call to one of its distant relatives.

PLOT PROGRESS

Impatience is not an attribute normally associated with gardening, and I used to wait until the first frosts before harvesting any of my winter crops. But time rolls on, and they look so good by now that I sometimes find myself gathering the first swedes and sprouts this month to change my dinner menu – you can have enough of runner beans, you know! It will not be long before the first leeks join these 'new' vegetables on the plate, but I will try to hold off on the parsnips until they have had a nip of frost to sweeten their flavour. Summer is truly over in our household now.

Picking swedes

Great expectations

One plant that shrugs off the vagaries of our weather is my pumpkin. Well fed on nutrients stored in my compost heap, it roams freely all over the lower half of my plot. By now, hidden amongst this dense foliage, there is a scattering of fruits sitting there like large yellow balls of sunshine. I still give it a twice-weekly feed of wormery juice, and it seems to thrive on all this attention. It is a while yet to Hallowe'en, though, and its final harvesting time.

An experiment with tall peas is hopefully coming to a happy conclusion. Many weeks ago I was at another allotment site, and one of the allotmenteers introduced me to a variety from a heritage collection with the fascinating name of 'Tutankhamun'. They grew forever skywards and now, at over 8 feet (2.4 m) high, they look like a large hedge loaded with deep purple flowers and pods – not quite what I expected from a

packet of peas. The pods do not seem very big yet but when popped open reveal themselves full of very sweet, tasty green peas. As the pods still need more time to swell, these plants too are getting a twice-weekly feed of the wormery juice. So that piece of ground will have given me a crop of early potatoes *and* a promising late crop of peas, something I have never experienced before.

'Tutankhamun' peas

Talking of new experiences, the broad beans that I sowed as an experiment some weeks ago (see page 190) are full of flowers with plenty of bees busy pollinating them, so I can expect the pods to start growing soon. These late beans do not seem to suffer the nibbling by bean weevils that normally affects the spring batch, but the cool damp nights this time of year can give them an attack of chocolate spot disease. This does not hinder their progress, though, and all is on course for a late crop, another first for me and a change to my growing routine.

Broad bean flowers

More 'firsts'

One of my trial vegetables recently was celeriac, which looked very good by September with its tall green tops of celery-like leaves and swelling roots – not as big as I hoped but useful when lifted and turned into 'celery-substitute' soup. I cannot grow celery well, but this alternative provides the same flavour and then I can pretend that I have succeeded! These tasty roots can remain in the ground until the first frost, so it is worth waiting a few more weeks for this winter vegetable to grow a little larger.

The other experimental crop for me this year is the globe artichoke. This is a handsome plant with several leafy buds on the top, just about ready for harvesting. (In its first year the crop doesn't mature until September, but by next year it will have settled down to the usual midsummer harvest.) It will add another new dimension to our menus at home, although my wife is left with the task of seeking out the best recipes for using this gourmet crop. There's nothing like a challenge! For me vegetables are the spice of life, and it is never too late to expand the range of home-grown crops.

The greenhouse is the only place left on the plot now that is still fully productive in summer crops. My cucumbers have just about succumbed to the cooler September nights, but the tomatoes continue to provide a daily picking. The most glorious sight of all is my peppers as they steadily turn various wonderful, almost Technicolor shades. They take an age to develop the bright reds and oranges of full maturity, but those sweetest fruits of the crop are well worth the wait. Enjoy these late summer glories, for their days are numbered.

Picking peppers

The compost debate

All gardeners need well-made seed and potting composts in which to rear seedlings and to grow good healthy plants in pots and other containers. Once you could depend on the quality of bought mixtures, but in recent years there has been a lot of discussion about the poor condition of modern-day composts. I tend not to get involved in this argument because I have evolved a satisfactory home-made mixture of my own: I use multi-purpose compost but add a vital secret ingredient.

My two wormeries provide not only the nutrient-rich liquid I use for feeding my crops, but also super-rich compost as a by-product. I harvest this solid residue regularly to go into my own all-purpose compost mix (it is too precious and concentrated to spread on the ground). I blend one part of wormery compost with three parts bought multi-purpose compost, and find the result is the perfect medium for growing seedlings and for potting on to produce plants with a vigorous root structure and strong healthy growth, ready for planting out in the soil.

To keep production of this rich dark compost ingredient going all winter, I move my wormeries into the greenhouse, which keeps the worms hard at work. After the initial outlay for the wormery and its residents, its products are there for free in exchange for a steady supply of kitchen waste.

Drumming up carrots

Standing proudly on guard like sentinels outside my greenhouse door are two drums of August-sown carrots. They are just waiting there for the summer greenhouse inhabitants to cease their cropping and be cleared out, then they can be moved into warmer spots under cover. There they will continue to grow in the extra gentle heat to produce the long orange roots I look forward to for my Christmas dinner. Until then the carrots left out on the plot will continue to provide all my needs, so there is no panic just yet for the drums to be moved indoors. They are an important part of my growing plan, though, because carrots are the mainstay of many of our meals all the year round.

Moving carrot drums into the greenhouse

SEPTEMBER TASKS

Clearing ground

Soon there will be obvious signs that the main part of the harvest is drawing to a close as large patches of drab bare earth begin to appear erratically throughout the plot. However, these areas are soon turned over and transformed again with a little flexing of the back muscles. I use a fork to break the soil down finely as I have not finished sowing just yet, for green manures sown now will produce a lush green pasture that will protect the ground from the ravages of whatever the coming winter has to throw at it. The rye grasses in my seed mixture will hold on to the nutrients in the soil while the nitrogen-rich vetches help create an oasis of improved fertility.

Not everywhere is emptying, of course, because parsnips, swedes, leeks, Brussels sprouts and savoys still occupy some areas of the plot. The shorter days have slowed the growth of these winter crops, and now I wait for the first frost to enhance their flavour even as it ends the life of those summer crops still hanging on.

The end of my beans

The climbing French beans are long past their sell-by date and look a pitiful sight, so it is time to remove them from the landscape. Their topgrowth is light and strawy, and supplies useful material for aerating the compost heap. The canes can then be pulled up and stored away for another year, always under cover safe from the winter elements – if they are looked after well, they can be used again for many a long year.

With the cooler nights my runner beans too are getting old and tough, with yellow leaves and fat seeds forming in their last brown bulging pods. There was a time in my early gardening career when I would religiously collect these seeds to sow for next year's crop. In those days the only bean grown on our allotments was 'Scarlet Emperor' and everyone saved their own seed – the bees that flew from one plant to another would be keeping the strain pure with no risk of cross-fertilization. On the modern allotment there must be dozens of different varieties, and if you collect the seeds they could well be of the 'Heinz 57' variety.

But old habits die hard, and I cannot resist popping these pods and filling my shirt pocket with the large swollen seeds. I take them home, empty them out on to a piece of kitchen roll, and leave them to dry out. Then into a paper bag they go and are kept dry until next season. These will be used as reinforcements to fill any gaps in my rows if there are failures among the several packets of new seed I will be buying.

Planning next year's crops

As the plot empties and the season moves on to an end, it is a good time to plan next year's crop rotation. I have this year's plan hanging in the shed, but being a greedy gardener I tend to stick something extra anywhere left vacant as early crops are harvested, and the plan sometimes goes a little awry.

So before the remnants of this year's plants are removed and while my ageing brain cells still remember where everything went, it is out with an A4 pad to work out the best crop rotation and then commit the new plan to paper. If I study where this year's crops were grown, I can move them to fresh ground and minimize the pests and diseases that affect certain plants while also helping maintain perfect growing conditions for them.

Then, on a day when the ground says 'keep off – too wet', I walk around the paths with my plan and a handful of old canes to mark out roughly where each of the main crops is going to go next year. This makes it simpler during the winter months to carry out the appropriate preparation in each area to ensure the various plants will be big, strong, healthy and, above all, productive.

Time to string onions

This year's maincrop onions that have been drying off on the greenhouse staging are now ready to be strung up. I believe that onions stored as strings or ropes in a cool airy environment last the long winter much better than those kept on shelves. And the full strings always look a splendid sight hanging in rows from the rafters of the shed.

I pick the biggest, tie it at the base of a length of string, and then weave the dried tops of the others in and out of the string above it, making sure the bunch is tight and not too heavy. Finally I loop the top of the string to hang it up, and then individual onions can be cut off as required.

Strung onions

A start on next year's crops

The planting season has not yet entirely ceased. A little brown box delivered to me at home this month, containing my winter onions and garlic, reawakens the gardener's familiar pleasure of planting.

These winter onions used to be called Japanese onions several years ago, and were a way of growing onions over the winter months to give an early crop the following June. The stored maincrop onions keep until late April to early May before the last remaining few start sending up fresh green shoots in their urge to grow again, and these winter varieties are intended to fill the gap before the new season's maincrop is ready.

So it is out with the fork to prepare the soil, adding a little dressing of dried horse manure or chicken manure, and then the onions are popped in. And there we have it, next year's crops under way already. The garlic meanwhile can remain in the shed for a few more weeks yet, and will not be planted until late October, on Hallowe'en as is my habit.

Sprout maintenance

My Brussels sprouts have had a great time under the protection of my insect net and they are like a small forest by now. The stems are filling out with firm young buttons, but I ought to wait a little longer before plucking some for my dinner. It is always best if they experience a touch of frost first to enhance their flavour, but with frosts arriving later every year and my beans finished I may be forced to harvest a few. Not too many – there is a long winter ahead when I can enjoy them, so I can wait!

It will not be long, though, before strong winds whip up through the valley, and these could wreak havoc with the tall, heavily laden plants, rocking them back and forth in the wet ground and loosening their roots. It is time to come to their aid, so I knock stout wooden battens into the ground, attach sturdy string and then weave it through the plants to hold them upright and keep their firm green sprouts from being covered in earth.

Gooseberry care

My gooseberry bush has lost most of its greenery and has gone to rest after giving me a bumper crop of berries for my tarts and fools. I never prune this productive bush severely, but merely give it a 'short back and sides'. First I remove any twisted or overlapping branches, and open up the centre of the bush to allow a free flow of air through the bush. Then I clip around the perimeter to give it a neat shape. This annual treatment seems enough to keep it in good heart, and it always rewards me well for this bit of TLC. Mind you, it is also extremely lucky to be growing just where I tip my manure from the trailer it is delivered in, and the bush gets all the dregs of manure I cannot scrape up!

Pruning the gooseberry bush

Raining leaves

While cleaning up the summer debris at the bottom of the plot my eye is caught by a silent shower of golden 'raindrops' as the trees start to shed their brown, gold and yellow leaves. Soon they will be cascading in torrents from the sky, carpeting the ground with autumn tints, and then the task of clearing them away will begin in earnest. To many this is an additional chore, but for the gardening faithful like me this is manna from heaven and a great soil improver.

I gather all my leaves, and those of many of my neighbours, and corral them in a wire netting enclosure to stop them whirling all over the place in the high autumn winds. There they slowly decompose into a rich brown soil improver, delivering benefits to next year's crops and making the seed bed a great place for germination and growth. Making leafmould is just another part of the life of a patient organic grower, turning waste into profit. Always be a little selective with your leaves, though, and only use the softer types, because larger coarse leaves take an age to break down.

Looking back

We never seem to leave nature to her own devices, learning the lessons of the past and working in harmony with her for our mutual benefit.

I was a gardener in the 1960s when along came Lindane and DDT. These were seen as saviours of our crops and would, it was thought, eliminate all those nasty pests that attacked them. What was not realized at the time was that they were totally indiscriminate and eliminated all our allies too. Then it was found that this lethal cocktail of insecticides was polluting the environment and building up a chemical time bomb in our soil.

It seems to me that we always want to play at being God and interfere with the laws of nature. But all too often this leads to catastrophic consequences with lasting detriment to the environment.

There, I have got that off my chest now! I can put away my soapbox and return to the tranquillity of my plot, where everything is at one with nature and all is in order.

SEPTEMBER IN A NUTSHELL

Key jobs for SEPTEMBER

- ✔ Harvest autumn raspberries.
- ✔ Watch out for those late cabbage white butterfly caterpillars.
- ✔ Continue harvesting greenhouse tomatoes, cucumbers and peppers.
- ✔ Keep preparing empty areas of soil and sowing green manure crops.
- ✔ Plant winter onions.

If you have time . . .

- ✔ Revisit your plan and finalize next year's crop rotation.

Looking ahead to OCTOBER

- ✔ Start to harvest the first winter leeks, swedes and parsnips.
- ✔ Plant garlic on the bewitching day of Hallowe'en.
- ✔ Open up and fill bean trenches with discarded compost and green waste from pots and baskets.
- ✔ Harvest pumpkins when the outer skin has toughened up and ripened.
- ✔ Tidy up the summer clutter in the shed.
- ✔ Prune autumn raspberries once cropping ends.

Late peppers

Thought for the month

As the poet says, autumn is the 'season of mists and mellow fruitfulness', which is a very apt description of the plot at this time of year. The days are definitely a lot chillier, and there is that tingle of coolness on your skin when you step into the garden in the early morning. There to greet you is a haze of low mist hugging the hillsides, but this is quickly chased away by the sun lying low in the morning sky.

The fruitfulness is all around. Crops are ripening before your very eyes, soaking up the weak sunlight to capture their full flavour, ready for long winter storage. The onions are gathered in, joining the garlic and shallots in the greenhouse to complete their drying process, and when ready will be strung up and hung in a cool, airy place to be nipped off the bunch as needed to add flavour to those winter dishes. Out on the plot marrows, squashes and pumpkins are still sunbathing to harden their skins before joining their fellow vegetables in the dry, frost-free shed.

Yes, fruitfulness is really with us now, and these stored treasures will provide some of our daily needs during those long, dark, barren months that lie ahead. What a great provider Mother Nature is!

OCTOBER

IT HAS FINALLY ARRIVED ON MY WELSH hillside – yes, this month usually brings a white covering of crystalline frost. And the first indication is that strange brightness that greets the new day. Just as night follows day, a night of frost is followed by bright azure sky and then, shortly afterwards, by that brilliant ball of yellow which soon gets to work on this coating of cold ice. Before your very eyes this melts away to reveal the tender summer foliage turned into a blackened soggy mass.

The first casualties are the larger leaves and fleshy stalks of the courgettes and squashes. Gone now are my late bonus yields from these prolific fruiters, leaving the winter crops to act out their role as 'toughs'. These will be all the better for the cold that turns their starches into sugars.

Any dry periods during this month enable me to get the allotment ready for its winter slumber. Not that there is much of my plot that is actually empty at any time of the year. Large blocks of winter vegetables take up much of the ground, while those areas where summer crops have been cleared are now green with my winter manures. This just leaves those patches where remaining summer vegetables have been finished by the frost, which I now need to clear and turn over, exposing the soil for the elements to break down into a fine tilth.

Towards the end of this month we reach that confusing moment when man interferes with time and the clocks 'fall back'. This takes a whole hour of useful daylight from the end of the day and transfers it to the morning. Why, I wonder? The total hours of daylight are already reducing steadily, so why do we need this disruptive readjustment of the clocks?

October's highlights

It's the time of year associated with ghosts and ghoulies as the bewitching day of Hallowe'en approaches. This has several significances in my gardening calendar.

The first is a reminder to plant my garlic (to ward off those silent vampires!) in the patch of ground I have already prepared with a coating of well-rotted manure. The large bulbs are split up into their individual cloves, with each being planted just beneath the surface. These will then have an adequate cold period in the soil to enable them to create a good root structure before their little green shoots burst through the surface in the new year.

Planting garlic

The second highlight is that it's time to harvest the vegetable closely associated with Hallowe'en, my pumpkin. This large bronze specimen is hollowed out by the younger members of the family to create a grotesque mask, which gives an appropriately evil appearance to our doorway when lit from within by a flickering candle.

For many years I grew the enormous variety 'Atlantic Giant'. The largest I ever produced weighed 13½ stone (190 kg), and this went off to a local charity to raise lots of money for their cause. No longer am I able to grow these giants, though, as they take up too much of my plot, which is why I always tried to 'borrow' the spare portion of someone else's plot to raise this monster of a plant.

But austere times have struck the allotments and everyone fills their plot to capacity with crops to feed the family. Still, I do manage to find room for a smaller variety of pumpkin, which keeps my granddaughter happy!

Salvage operation

Only the hardy still manage to survive out on the October plot, and the last super-cropper of summer, my courgettes, have come to an end and given me their final fruits. This vegetable is a winner on my plot, and one or two plants go a long way towards fulfilling my 'never buy veg' ambitions.

They have featured in a lot of meals in our household, while the surpluses have gone into chutneys and even jams, so it seems scant reward for all those long productive months that the rambling plants are finally pulled up and consigned to the compost heap. There are just a few last courgettes to take home and their lingering flavour to savour before it is time to readjust my taste buds ready for those winter vegetables.

With a wet end to the onion season, the bulbs may not have dried off fully, even after some time inside on the greenhouse staging. Unfortunately it can stay damp even in there, with the result that some of the onions decide to start growing again, pushing fresh green shoots out of their tops. These are no good for long-term storage and it is best to use them up quickly. Onions can be chopped and frozen, but at the moment the freezer is full of all those other vegetables, so there are often plenty of onion-based dishes on our menu this month. Waste not, want not!

Autumn tints

There is one bright oasis in the dank October days on my plot, and that is my chrysanthemums. They look splendid, with their vivid shades of red, orange, yellow and pink lighting up the gloom in defiance of the weather. These are not the large reflex and incurve varieties of the show bench, but the multi-headed spray type that will grace our hall and living room when I take them home at the end of a day tidying up the plot.

Autumn hues of the chrysanthemums

Tales from the plot

At last we can enter the allotments through our large metal gates without a major struggle with the chain and lock. For some years one of the posts has slowly sunk into the ground (I am sure the old colliery workings must run under our allotments), making life difficult for anyone trying to open the gate. But all is now well and back to normal. Dave H slogged and toiled to remove the sunken post after delving down several feet into the ground, and got it back in position – the slide moves freely, the lock fits the original hole, and access is a piece of cake again. No more expletives in future from members struggling to enter.

Talking of gates, 'Bob the Builder' is certainly ringing the changes on our somewhat dull hillside. Now he has introduced a little bit of ancient Rome! He has erected two posts and a gate leading to his plot, and on one of the posts has installed a bust of a Roman emperor. The way in now is like walking into a gladiators' arena – though you needn't be ready to do battle with anything more dangerous than a few weeds.

It is hard to believe that he has yet more projects for his new plot. He had a few blocks left over from one of his paths and decided that, if he obtained a few more, he could make a further addition to the plot. So far he has already bought a shed, constructed a conservatory-type greenhouse, made raised beds and laid 'proper' concreted paths. Now he is building into the bank at the top of his plot what can only be described as a nuclear bunker.

This is the ultimate in accessories, and we all feel much safer knowing we shall soon have the protection of this latest must-have allotment structure. There is no doubt in my mind that when Bob finally hangs up his gardening shoes there will be a mass of applications to move to this plot, improved with so many features never before seen in my fifty years of gardening here!

Coffee break

Something strange is happening down on Anthony's plot, where suddenly lots of large drawers from filing cabinets have appeared. What on earth is he going to do – file his seeds alphabetically? No, he has found a way of recycling them to create a raised bed, just one more example of ingenuity at work with discarded goods. I suppose he will grow the crops in his new bed in order, from artichokes, beetroot and carrots, right down to zinnias. Now that would be a challenge!

A crisis that could have had catastrophic effects occurred recently when Albie's stove sprang a gas leak. Café closed until further notice!

It required urgent action, of course, so a team of experts was called in. Albie's son fitted a new length of pipe to the stove, but in doing so broke the regulator. Russell V was then called upon but couldn't fix it. So John P came to the rescue, despite having problems of his own with his shed, and produced a new regulator. Gas on tap once more.

But Albie was not happy as he could hear gas leaking in the café. Me to the scene this time. After tightening the pipe fully I could still hear the gas leaking. Scratching my head in bewilderment I then realized he had left one of the burner taps slightly open. So many willing hands made the gas light work, and the crisis was finally over. Time to celebrate with a brew!

There are subtle changes taking place in the growing programmes on this hillside, with more varied crops being grown there all the time.

We had an unexpected tasting session on the bench outside Albie's café the other day, for example, after Keith came across from his plot bearing a tray laden with bunches of black grapes. The succulent tempting bunches were soon being sampled by all and sundry, and deliciously sweet they were, too. Now we are all waiting impatiently to experience the hillside flavour of the wine they are going to be turned into.

For some reason Albie went out and bought a folding trolley, which now sits in pride of place in his café, although there is no work for it to do. 'It might come in handy soon,' he said, but who knows when – possibly he is anticipating the arrival of Château de Keith!

A lorry turned up at the gate one Saturday morning carrying another load of cast-off goodies for the thrifty allotmenteers – it is almost a regular occurrence. This one contained scaffolding boards and some scaffolding poles, both short and long. These are perfect for use on the plot: the poles support tall plants, while the boards make perfect edging, or planks we can walk on to avoid making deep holes with our heels when the ground is wet.

All this free bounty soon went as everyone could find a use for it. But just then Bolts realized that he could do with one more of the short boards and came over, asking, 'Does anyone have a short plank to spare?'

The swift reply was 'Yes!', and we all looked at Tony who was sitting there, quietly minding his own business, on the bench. 'Will he do?' we all said in unison.

To quote a well-known public figure from the past, he 'was not amused'.

PLOT PROGRESS

I usually manage to take a break this month when the pressure is off at last, but like all holidays it is quickly over. I am soon back on my Welsh hillside and it is then I notice how many changes there have been on the plot; when you are a regular visitor – and by that I mean daily! – changes are subtle and not so noticeable. Even so, I am surprised at this late stage in the season just how full my plot still seems.

The winter green manures thrive in the damp conditions at this time of year and by now create a very green oasis on the plot despite the steadily shortening daylight hours. None of the winter vegetables will have missed me one bit; they just continue growing in my absence. Besides these my summer root crops are still in residence. I don't lift and store my remaining carrots and beetroot, but leave these out on the plot for a bit longer.

The maincrop carrots are steadily depleting. I have already harvested a large tray of them, and these have been chopped and bagged up in the freezer to give me a supply of carrots later on in winter. The rest enjoy the extra protection of their Enviromesh covering, even though the last of the carrot flies has long gone, and with a bit of luck I should go on harvesting from under this frame for a couple more months yet.

All this variety makes my plot seem interesting the year round, and gardeners who only plan for summer crops are missing out on the pleasures of the complete gardening calendar.

Back to a feast

One of the first things I do on my return is to set about harvesting a basket of fresh vegetables to replenish my diminished larder.

There appears to be little sign of really hard frost in our valley and I cannot wait any longer to savour my parsnips. In a wet autumn those roots in the soil tend to suffer and their crowns develop canker, a fungal

Harvesting maincrop carrots

disease that spreads with ease across an allotment and thrives in a wet late summer. As in previous years, though, I made a back-up plan and have sown four large drums with parsnips, which always produce long, beautifully clean white roots. I may have to abandon growing parsnips in the soil in future and confine them instead to drums filled with a mixture of horticultural sand and compost.

To celebrate my homecoming I take my spade and carefully dig two parsnips from the batch in the earth. Their long growing period has made their tap root search deep in the soil for water and nourishment, so they don't give up without a bit of a struggle. After some careful manoeuvring on my part they slowly slide and release their grip in the ground to reveal promisingly long, broad-shouldered and tapered roots. A quick swill in my water barrels and I have two fine parsnips to roast and coat in honey for my Sunday lunch.

Leeks

Having assembled the autumn flavours of parsnips, swedes and sprouts, it is the turn of my leeks, standing there proud and healthy in their long blanching tubes – just one will be enough to add an exquisite and distinctive flavour to the dish. Once it has been lifted I have the difficult job of removing the thick shank from the tube, but a quick dip in the water butt soon lubricates the tight tube and it slides off easily to reveal a fine long white shank.

No need to rush to the supermarket: we will soon be feasting on home-grown produce again!

Tending the soil

Many of our plot-holders are still very traditional about the winter care of their plots. They turn all the ground over roughly in autumn with a spade, leaving large clods for the elements to work on. Then they lime large areas of the plot, which transforms the landscape into something like a great Arctic waste.

Personally I find that the winters are getting warmer and wetter, so this traditional autumn liming serves no purpose – our continual downpours wash much of this lime away and by next spring its benefits are gone. I find it much more effective to lime the ground in spring to retain the full impact of the alkaline dressing, which gives added zest to the soil.

Gardening is a lifelong learning experience and every day something new comes along to enrich our knowledge. Just recently, for example, I learned a new technique of winter cultivation that was widely used (so I was reliably informed) in Victorian times.

If you dig a trench about 2 feet (60 cm) deep and line it with fresh strawy horse manure, you can create a hot bed. Once you have heaped the soil back into the trench, the manure beneath starts to give off heat as it rots down. Hardy crops like kale or winter cabbage planted on top of the trench can benefit greatly from the gentle warmth at their toes, enhancing the speed at which they grow. It is a bit like putting an electric blanket in your bed during the cold winter nights.

So now it is off to find a source of fresh stable manure and put the theory to the test.

IN THE GREENHOUSE

It is a great comfort to know that when those heavy rains start to fall you can always retreat to the dry of the greenhouse, where the mood this month is Hot! Hot! Hot!

That is nothing to do with the temperature, I should add, but the abundance of vivid colour after a few warm and sunny autumn days have given rise to a bumper crop of red peppers. I thought I would be eating lots of the less tasty green ones, but that is not the case in a fine October – it seems that, like us, their skin quickly reddens after several hours of unprotected sunbathing. Happily so, because stuffed red peppers are my favourite and any surplus of this tasty crop will be housed in the freezer to act as winter warmers.

Even though the plants are near the end of their lives, brilliant scarlet late peppers can be hanging there aplenty, all at their peak and ready to harvest. The chillies look like long pipes, their bright colouring a tempting foretaste of those tongue-tingling flavours they add to my curries and hot winter dishes. Beware, though, I also have some little orange ones hidden amongst the others – a bite of one of these would send you scuttling to the nearest water barrel to douse the heat!

So even if it's cold outside, I am greeted this month by a little bit of the Mediterranean in the greenhouse.

Spring strawberries

Many weeks ago now I cleaned up my strawberry beds and cut off the old foliage once the plants had finished cropping. Since then they have made plenty of new growth, however, and sent out many more runners, some of these even flowering again, so before winter sets in they will need further sorting out to get them into good shape to give another bumper harvest at the height of next summer.

Some of the strongest runners I find will be potted up and placed in the greenhouse to give me a few very early pickings. These 'babies' are planted in deep 5-inch (13 cm) pots in a good multi-purpose compost and then placed under my greenhouse staging, where they are given a minimal amount of watering, to keep them almost dry and free from fungal diseases. Come early spring they are moved on to the staging and given a good high-potash feed to spur them into action and form new growth. They will hopefully fruit by late spring, a month ahead of their outdoor cousins, and give me an early taste of what lies ahead.

Beyond the greenhouse door

During early spring I was given some Jerusalem artichoke tubers, which I planted alongside one of my greenhouse water butts. Then I promptly forgot about them.

Artichokes

Artichoke tubers

Towards the end of spring a mass of green shoots appeared through the soil, and now the amazing plants stand more than 7 feet (2.1 m) tall and look very impressive. But suddenly I am getting fears about this reckless planting as many gardeners have told me since that these artichokes are 'thugs' and worse even than Japanese knotweed for persistence and spread.

Now what do I do? Should I throw caution to the winds and wait to harvest some of these new tubers for their unique culinary qualities, or do I follow everyone else's advice to destroy the plants immediately? I suspect the former will apply, just so that I can at least taste the fruits of my labour – if the flavour is not to my liking, then this planting will certainly be for the chop.

Also outside are some bins, now sadly empty, that were home to carrots earlier in the season. These are full of a good mixture of compost and sand, but there is no way I can use this mixture again for next year's carrot crop. The greenhouse borders are due to be changed this year as soon as the last tomatoes are cleared, and this carrot bin mix will make a great addition to the replenished borders, so now I shall empty this perfect soil improver into bags to store for later use. Then the bins can be cleaned out ready for filling with fresh mix next spring to grow another early carrot crop. Crop rotation on a small scale!

OCTOBER TASKS

Liberating leeks

My leeks are looking perfect by this month, almost demanding that I release them from the soil with my fork. Dry weather over the past few months can have a major beneficial effect on this crop, keeping the plants free from the rust pustules that often disfigure them in a wet autumn.

To increase the length of their blanch I carefully enclose my leeks in plastic sleeves during early summer, so I have to ease each one gently from the soil, slide its plastic sleeve over the roots and, voilà, there is a perfect specimen of a leek with over 10 inches (25 cm) of pure white shank – ideal for braising. Before taking the harvest home to grace my dinner plate, I wash the empty sleeves with a bottle brush and store them away in clean condition for future use. What a great use of recycled tubing that once carried our telephone wires!

Harvesting leeks

Time for garlic

It seems an age since something was actually planted on my plot but this month is the moment I have been waiting for to plant my garlic cloves. My advice is always buy your garlic from a British source and do not be tempted to plant those beautiful white bulbs sold in supermarkets – these have been grown in warmer climes and are not accustomed to the variables of our fickle climate, and sometimes they carry viral diseases too.

Prepare the bed with plenty of added rich compost, then split the bulbs into their individual cloves and plant the largest ones with their tips just below the surface (the small ones that are left I plant in a clump; these will make smaller bulbs, ready for planting next year). And there we are: the garlic will receive the cool conditions it needs to make a good root system before its grass-like shoots appear above the soil, and I turn the page of a new chapter of next year's growing season to begin the cycle again.

Giving in to temptation

My tall sprouts are laden with solid green balls, and I am overcome by the irresistible temptation to harvest some. The best way is to pick from the bottom up, only enough for the meal, and then leave the rest on the stalk where they remain at their tastiest and very fresh. Whilst picking I take the opportunity to remove any dead lower leaves from the ground and from the lower regions of the stalk. This clear-up disposes of the potential cover for marauding slugs, which would hide in this fallen debris, just waiting for the chance to nibble the lower sprouts before you harvest them. Do not be tempted to remove any green leaves, though, as these give some protection to the forming sprouts.

This is also the chance to check the supports knocked in last month before the wild autumn winds could wreak havoc among the plants. Some old off-cuts of battens left over from a roofing job are perfect for extra reinforcement and usually free! Knock one alongside every loose top-

Staking sprouts

heavy plant and tie it in with stout cord – then the sprout stalks will not be rocked about and brought crashing to the ground in strong wind or heavy rain. Roll on the days of winter when they are encrusted with white frost and at their tastiest, and my fingers tingle whilst harvesting them.

Now that I have started to harvest them, the protective netting is removed from over the sprouts to allow me easy access. But there is one crop that must remain in the safety of its net cage all winter long, and that is my batch of spring cabbages. These have grown well and made plenty of lush, leafy growth and this will certainly tempt the pigeons to have a free feed when there's nothing else around. I'm not taking any chances!

Feeding hungry beans

This year's runner beans have completed their life cycle, the tops have been removed to the compost heap, and now is a good time to examine the canes before storing them away over winter. After a thrifty few years in the soil some of them are going rotten at the base, which means the end of their useful life as bean poles although they can be shortened to support my chrysanthemums next season. Any that have gone weak along their whole length are still of use when cut into short sticks for marking rows of sown seeds. A cane has to work hard on my plot throughout its long life before crumbling away to dust, and my only regret now is that I have to spend some of my cash to buy a few new ones – oh, how I envy those lucky people who can get bean supports from a regularly coppiced willow plantation.

Now I have the important job of replenishing the fertility of this bean row. I rarely move my runner beans as part of my rotation, but I do prepare the area with special care. Two cord lines are stretched along the row and a spade's-depth trench is opened out about 18 inches (45 cm) wide. This is filled with all the spent topgrowth and compost from my hanging baskets and pots, about 4 inches (10 cm) deep, which I then cover with my magic ingredient of 4 inches (10 cm) of well-rotted horse manure. The trench is left open for three weeks to allow the contents time to settle and then it is back-filled, leaving a high mound of soil that slowly sinks down in the long winter months. This is the perfect rich, moisture-retentive foundation for those thirsty, hungry beans next season.

Autumn cleaning time

Any brief interludes of glorious weather in autumn must be used wisely, so I try to get on with cleaning up the plot. Annual weeds are on payback time and can be dug into the soil where they will decompose and give a little richness back, so that at last they are put to a useful purpose. Perennial weeds, on the other hand, need removing and disposing of well away from the plot – no compost heap for them! All those empty pots and trays that are lying around the plot make the ideal winter home for snails, which gather in any of these safe little havens they find left around, so tidy up and don't make life easy for them.

Tidying the plot

Then it is time to turn my attention to my garden shed, which has become untidy and rather full as my props and nets are removed from the plot for winter storage. It also houses all those seed trays and pots cleared out of the greenhouse and off the plot. I look at the mass of material that I store, wonder why I need it all, and start clearing in earnest, determined to throw some of it away. But thriftiness always gets in the way and most of the stuff has a use, so it stays! Still, at the end of the clearing exercise I can at least get into the shed and close the door.

Tidying the shed

Tidying the shed is a good time to check those winter vegetables stored there. The potatoes are snug in their sacks, but it takes only one bad potato to ruin a whole sackful. I tip them out into trays, remove any that look dubious and either use them up quickly or, if in doubt, throw them away in the rubbish bin (*not* the compost heap!). The onions also need looking over, especially after a very wet late summer when some may not have dried well and could be showing signs of mould. They too can be used in the kitchen before they rot, and removing them from the strings will usually save the rest of the crop.

Looking back

It is Hallowe'en this month, or – in modern Americanized idiom – 'trick or treat' time. In days long past there were no such things as pumpkins on our allotments and we had to make do with a large hollowed-out swede. My father grew lots of these, which were turned to good use on Hallowe'en as carved lanterns, and I had many friends in those childhood times who were grateful for my father's gardening prowess in providing them with swedes on time and free of charge.

Why have all these old customs disappeared from festivals like this one, which we called 'ducking apple night' in my youth? This was the time when kids gathered in the kitchens of neighbours' houses and, while blindfolded and with hands behind their backs, tried to take a bite out of an apple swinging on a string – or alternatively tried without using their hands to bite apples bobbing about in a bowl of water. Things were so much simpler then.

OCTOBER IN A NUTSHELL

Key jobs for OCTOBER

- ✔ Get those garlic cloves planted for next year's early crop.
- ✔ Check crops in storage such as onions and potatoes to remove any going bad.
- ✔ Harvest Jerusalem artichokes.
- ✔ Check the stakes supporting sprouts to ensure they are still firm.

If you have time . . .

- ✔ Plant up a few strawberry runners and bring into the greenhouse for a late spring crop.

Looking ahead to NOVEMBER

- ✔ Clean up the rhubarb bed and select a new crown for early forcing.
- ✔ Lift chrysanthemum stools and bring indoors for cuttings in the New Year.
- ✔ Bring wormeries into the greenhouse to encourage the worms to keep on producing that rich compost.
- ✔ Harvest all winter crops as they are required.

Checking sprouts

Thought for the month

While pondering on my next year's seed purchases, I was reading a report from a well-known consumer watchdog about the poor germination of modern seeds. As an allotment keeper of many decades who has sown seeds for more years than I care to mention, I can endorse that opinion to some degree.

Over forty years ago there were very few vegetable varieties and the same kinds were grown year on year. It seemed as though we just buried them in the soil and, within the stated germination time, up popped these little seed leaves in abundance. Today there are dozens of different varieties of every vegetable, many of them F1 hybrids, and these little prima donnas of the modern seed world need so much more cosseting and special care to ensure adequate germination.

I now start many of my sowings in trays and pots in the warm surroundings of the greenhouse before exposing them to the vagaries of the Welsh weather. Seeds of root crops like carrots I do sow outside, but not directly into the soil – first I line the drill with seed compost and then, after sowing the seeds, cover them with more of the same compost. This equivalent of sowing in a seed tray gives a much higher degree of success in the germination stakes.

It seems that more care and attention has to be lavished on these new kids on the block to make them grow, so change our sowing habits we must!

NOVEMBER

THE DARKNESS MAY BE GATHERING momentum rapidly, but work out on the plot continues for the seasoned allotmenteer. Bring on a good frost, I say, and then I can tuck into more of those winter vegetables.

I remember the days when autumn seemed to start properly at the end of September. You could more or less expect a sharp frost that would quickly put paid to those summer crops, and in a single night of sub-zero temperatures the dahlias were turned to pulp.

To the north and east of my plot the hills certainly look very drab now in their covering of autumnal bracken with its light brown foliage. Where have the vibrant green hillsides of the summer gone? It doesn't seem that long ago that the well-known phrase 'how green was my valley' was an apt description. When traditionally cold weather does strike and produce beautiful white frosty mornings on cue, it brings joy to a gardener's heart to arrive at the plot and find it glistening with white crystals. This frosty coating looks like diamonds as the sun's rays are reflected from it, though it soon vanishes in the faint warmth that is all the weak sunshine has left to offer.

Recently, however, mild weather has often lasted into November, allowing for late bonus harvests of squash and beans and ripening the peppers in the greenhouse. The unseasonable warmth may also trick leeks into bolting and encourage so much growth that I will have spring cabbage for dinner before Christmas. But one or two Novembers have seen heavy snow. Climate change certainly keeps us gardeners on our toes.

November always opens with a bang in the form of Guy Fawkes Night, when a small bonfire on the plot will go unnoticed by neighbouring inhabitants. The days of smouldering fires all autumn are long gone, and I for one welcome the change in the way waste material is used. Most allotment holders compost their waste these days, but occasionally there is an amount of woody material that does not decompose well. A quick burn-up will get rid of these twiggy bits and give you a little natural potash in return – leave the ash to cool, then store it for a few months and it will make a super feed for your fruit bushes. They love it!

Bonfire

Taking stock

The colder November weather usually means that the pumpkin vine that dominated the lower area of my plot is no more than a mass of collapsing foliage by now. All this green waste can be gathered up and piled high on the two-year-old compost heap the plant has smothered for some months. That will release the contents of the heap at last, in perfect condition for supplying the nutrients to my plot in future months. I will miss that rambling giant, though, as it has given me hours of pleasure watching its massive fruits swell!

If the season doesn't suit them my leeks are liable to find themselves under constant threat. Wet, mild weather may bring on an attack of rust – more disfiguring than disastrous – while excessive warmth can prompt some to form large flowerheads among their tops, in the mistaken belief that winter is over and spring has arrived. These need digging up for use straight away because their centres are now likely to be hard and of little use in the kitchen.

Similarly purple sprouting broccoli, normally a reliable winter and early spring cropper, can throw numerous little precocious spears. These will make a change from the sprouts that tend to dominate our cooked meals in late autumn. I find more and more plants are doing strange things to keep us old gardeners in a state of uncertainty, and the weather is certainly one thing that makes this hobby so pleasurable in its constant surprises.

Tales from the plot

On every allotment site you'll find plenty of people who are willing to lend a helping hand to other plot-holders who might be struggling. But there are always some members who go that extra mile.

This morning Jeff was walking in and spotted Wayne L moving a load of manure that had just been delivered to his plot. Wayne has not been well of late and without any prompting Jeff picked up his fork and rapidly moved the heap on to Wayne's plot. Job done, he walked off, pleased to be of assistance to another member. Just a simple thanks was reward enough for this kindly deed. This is how allotment life will always be.

Carl walked in the gate the other day carrying some garlic bulbs he had bought.

'When do I plant these?' he asked.

'They should have gone in at the end of October, usually on Hallowe'en,' was our immediate response.

'Am I too late then?' he almost pleaded.

'No,' I replied. 'Take a chance and plant them now. The ground's not too cold yet.'

And off he went to plant his precious crop.

Shortly afterwards, his cloves of garlic duly planted, he went home, only to return a little while later with two slices of corned beef pie, made by his girlfriend Gail, as a reward. So there we sat, Albie and I, in the warmth of the café-cum-greenhouse and enjoyed that feast along with a hot mug of coffee. Thanks, Carl and Gail, for making two old men very contented.

A few weeks earlier I had arrived at the allotments with my own garlic cloves in an otherwise empty pot in the boot of my car, together with a large bag of kitchen waste that I had collected for my compost bins.

Struggling to carry both, I put the pot of garlic inside the bag, but before I reached my plot I was distracted and went to get something from the store shed. I then walked down the plot and tipped this bag of waste into my green Dalek-like compost bin.

After I had gone off to start planting the garlic I realized that I had tipped it all in with the compost, so I had to hunt down a pair of gloves and then lean deep into the bin to retrieve the cloves and pot from the slimy rotting waste – one of those gardening jobs that started out as a simple five-minute task but eventually ran into more than an hour. I must stop getting these senior moments or my plot will never be up to date!

Having collected all those now messy cloves together, I found the ground was rather wet, so I would need a stout plank to avoid making deep footprints in the sodden soil. I have some very long full-length scaffolding boards, but this time I was only going to plant short rows.

The plank

I shouted up to Brian to ask if he had a smaller plank I could use, which he duly gave me, but when I laid it across the planting area it turned out to be a little short.

'Is it all right?' he enquired.

'No,' I replied, 'it's about four inches too short.'

'Turn it around, then,' he said, 'it's only short at one end.'

One morning last week I had the whole of the allotments to myself.

The clouds hung low over the hillsides and a gentle misty rain was falling as I arrived at my normal time, only to find the gate still locked and chained. This was quite unusual because I am seldom the first there. I walked the length of the allotments, but not a regular in sight. Even after I'd spent an hour or so in my greenhouse, nobody had come through the gate.

It was an eerie experience for me to be alone there, and I cannot remember the last time that was the case. As it was too damp to work outside I finally packed up and went home. My wife was shocked to see me come back so soon and thought I was ill. I didn't dare tell her I was lonely on the plot, with no coffee or anyone to chat to, and that was the reason for my early homecoming!

When I arrived at the plot to find the ground so wet I could almost see the 'Keep Off!' signs, I decided to start my new project. My corral of fleece to protect the carrots from their dreaded root fly enemy had failed after summer winds and heavy rain breached the usually effective barrier, letting the marauders into my crop where they wreaked havoc among the roots.

But they would not manage it next year! I had some strong battening donated by Dave H, so I commenced making sturdy frames that would slip over the carrot rows. This could then be draped all over with Enviromesh (a much stronger protective screen than fleece), which would be held firmly in place and thus safely enclose my carrot crop. 'Keep Out!' was the order of the day for carrot root flies after that.

Covering carrots with fleece

Every second year I dig out the soil in my greenhouse borders to replace it with a fresh growing medium. This task now falling due, I set to digging and emptied four wheelbarrow loads of the good fertile soil that had housed my tomatoes on to the area where next year's carrot crop is going to reside – it makes a fabulous bed for those long orange roots to delve into. On the fifth load my barrow, which has been in the Walton gardening fraternity for decades and was used by my father before me, gave up the ghost and fell apart, the top becoming completely detached from the frame.

I examined the damage, which to me looked way beyond repair. However, Dai came to the rescue, told me to leave it by his greenhouse and said he would see if he could fix it. So time will tell if this antique barrow will see service again or go to another place – no, not the wheelbarrow cemetery in the sky but the local rag and bone man! Undeterred, I borrowed Albie's barrow and the greenhouse border was soon empty.

Allotments are more sociable places than they were years ago, the sheds converted into regular warm meeting places of like minds, with all the mod cons of home. There are gas stoves to help provide those welcoming cups of beverage all year round, comfortable chairs and facilities for producing anything from a piece of toast to a bacon butty during an hour of stimulating or thoughtful conversation.

It is not all gardening related. The troubles of the United Nations, for example, and many other world problems can be solved in the congenial surroundings typical of these places, and answers to many questions are always forthcoming. But unfortunately they fall on deaf ears beyond the plots, and all this wisdom is wasted! How much more contented the world we live in might be if the rules governing it were the same as those on an allotment.

There is no theft amongst members. It is a caring, sharing community ready to help anyone who needs it, and no one leaves the allotment without a generous donation of vegetables if they have failed with their own crop. Money is not the driving force because the good old-fashioned system of barter is still the predominant currency, and most surpluses of produce can be exchanged to meet the needs of all.

There is one place where money must change hands, and that is in the purchase of seeds, but even then the thrifty allotmenteer has tricks up his sleeve. Bulk buying can usually bring great discounts, so seed requirements are all combined into one group order, leading to savings of up to fifty per cent. Seed potatoes can be bought in sacks and shared out among the many plot-holders to bring about a significant reduction in cost. This manner of buying requires a great deal of trust among the various members, of course, once again bringing to the fore the essential good nature of allotmenteers.

There is much that can be learned from this way of life. The need to spend wisely is a creed by which the gardener lives, for example. There is also the willingness to make good use of many discarded objects and materials that society glibly throws away. This diverts the stuff from landfill, even as – most importantly in these austere times – it helps keep our money in our pockets.

The motto of a dedicated allotmenteer is 'never buy what can be reused or borrowed, and where spending is necessary use your money wisely and the harvests will be both plentiful and rich'. This philosophy has kept me in good stead not only in my gardening activities but also in my life in general.

There are many people on our waiting list, just as there are for allotments the length and breadth of the country, and recently a very rare event occurred here: a plot became vacant. One of our members, who has been cultivating two plots for over thirty years, decided that one was now enough.

I can hear the outcry, 'Why should one person have two plots, when there are people waiting to become newly fledged allotmenteers?' But what about all those years when allotments were in decline? No one was interested in 'grow your own' then, preferring to pop to the supermarket and purchase a plastic bag containing clean, almost tasteless vegetables.

It was people like our long-term member who kept allotment life going. I took on ten plots myself in the 1960s just to keep the allotments from becoming derelict and a prime target for developers (mind you, having ten plots certainly made crop rotation much easier!). It is too late to protest once this fertile land has vanished under concrete and tarmac and is lost forever.

Having waiting lists is a great incentive for committees and local council officers to ensure that plots are cultivated and well used. Some people (fortunately but a few) have an allotment just to be in vogue and be able to brag about it at the local pub. This piece of paradise is too precious for that and can provide a genuinely keen gardener with many happy hours in the pursuit of growing their own tasty produce.

I am secretary of our allotments, and I cannot wait to make someone happy at the prospect of having their own plot and seeing their dream come true.

In my early days on the plot there was always a safe way to take care of pests and diseases, and furthermore the solution was usually to be had for nothing – no complicated chemicals and sprays which cost the earth, but natural substances that were freely available. Careful planting and crop rotation were common practice, and as a result plants grew strong and pest predators roamed freely. Everyone encouraged the same good conditions, so potential transfer of pests and diseases was minimized.

The soil, which is the life blood of all plants, was never abused but tended well and lovingly cared for. It was fed with home-made composts and plenty of manure from stables where the horses were kept on a bed of straw – no hint of the wood shavings or chemical cleaners often used in stables now.

Those were the days of coal fires and plenty of soot from overworked chimney sweeps who were only too glad to pass this waste product on to receptive gardeners. When weathered well this potent fertilizer was a valuable and free tonic for any crop, and also proved a good deterrent against pests of onions and broad beans.

What can modern electric and gas fires provide for the garden? Nothing!

PLOT PROGRESS

Where are we heading in these modern times of climate change? Here we are, right at the end of autumn, and yet some years many summer crops have yet to yield to winter. Plot-holders who planted their runner beans late may still be picking handfuls of tasty young beans, while my green manure can be standing 10 inches (25 cm) or more high and still growing.

I have no complaints about this extended season, mind: it can give me treats beyond my wildest dreams, with red peppers filling the greenhouse and still more pear-shaped butternut squashes out on the plot. My spring cabbages make so much tender green growth these days that the net intended to protect them from the plunging beaks of the local wood pigeons is straining to contain the unusually lush crop. If they do not slow down soon they will be forming the basis of my December dinners.

The winter onions that should also be appearing dormant at this time of year are often sending up long green shoots, instead of just making plenty of good root structure beneath the surface without much growth above ground. A hard frost will shock both of these crops if they continue with so much unseasonable growth.

A really cold snap this time of year will put paid to the last of the summer plants, all of which are blackened by the effect of the sunlight on the frosted leaves, but there are many benefits. Winter vegetables will taste that much sweeter as a result of being frosted, while the last lingering pests of summer will be driven to seek cover far from the Arctic blast. Who knows, even the gardeners' worst enemies – the slugs and snails – may finally stop feeding on our precious winter crops.

IN THE GREENHOUSE

Refurbishing time

Not even the wettest of Novembers, when the last full dry day on my hillside here is a distant memory, can deter me from making my daily visits: I can always focus my attention this month on preparing the greenhouse for next year.

I always plant my greenhouse crops directly into the borders as I am not a fan of growing in buckets or growbags, especially when it comes to tomatoes. The problem with confined containers is that watering has to be carried out very efficiently, and the surface of growbags in particular can form a hard crust so that water runs off and the roots dry out. This leads to blossom end rot and very poor quality fruit. In the border, on the other hand, the roots can spread out well, making watering and feeding much simpler.

The downside of this border growing is that every two years I am faced with the task of emptying out all the soil and replacing it completely with a new growing medium. This avoids a build-up of disease and is really a form of soil rotation, albeit by moving one lot of growing medium out of the greenhouse and then bringing a new lot inside. With the greenhouse all but empty this month I can set about this task with gusto.

Winter precautions

With the greenhouse clean and ready for next year, it is time to prepare for any cold snap that might appear. So out with my roll of bubble wrap – which I did not buy as it was found outside a house after a big item had been delivered. I line the windows with this super heat-retaining material to make secondary double glazing, fix it in place with drawing pins and drape it over the wires which in summer support my cucumber plants as they trail along the roof. And lo, my patented hot bench is prepared, an insulated

Lining the greenhouse

area to house my chrysanthemum stools and protect my New Year sowings, when I keep a small paraffin lamp alight inside this warm tent.

Then I can take a fork and a pair of secateurs to rescue the forlorn-looking chrysanthemums from their outdoor rows. Their woody tops are removed and when dry can be burned for potash (they are not ideal material for the compost heap), and then each is carefully labelled and placed into its individual pot. These come into the greenhouse for potting in my special mix of three parts multi-purpose compost to one part worm compost, and stay snug and safe in the greenhouse until January, when a little gentle heat under the staging will encourage them to send up new shoots – a free source of new plants for next year!

NOVEMBER TASKS

I am still paying my daily visits to the plot, even though it is now approaching its dormant period. While I am driving the few miles to the site my mind is planning the jobs that need to be done during the morning session. And what a waste of brain space that always turns out to be!

As I walk the plot on my arrival – my usual routine – a diverse range of tasks stick out like a sore thumb and demand to be done. I start one of them as it is only a 'quickie', but after several of these unplanned jobs the morning has contrived to slip away. Gardening is always about planning to get the best results, but somehow planning the sequence of tasks is always overruled by necessity.

Be adventurous!

November is the only month in my calendar where I am not actually sowing anything. As evenings in the garden are off the agenda now, it is a good time to settle down with the vast array of seed catalogues that drop on to the doormat, and contemplate next season's sowings.

The beautifully illustrated catalogues peddle dreams, coaxing us all into buying more seed than we need while forgetting that, for all our aims and ambitions, our crops will not necessarily look as good as those shown in the photographs. I stick to many of the varieties that have proved most successful down the years on my plot, because my main reason for having an allotment is to feed myself.

But it would be totally boring to grow all the same things year in, year out. The fun side of gardening is to let your sense of adventure shine through and buy a few packets of something you have not grown before. Some of these will fail, inevitably, but any that succeed might surprise your taste buds or, if nothing else, will make a talking point on the plot next summer. Gardening has its serious side, but it is the freedom to grow whatever you want on your plot that encourages the diversity of the allotment community.

Rejuvenating old rhubarb

To achieve my objective of enjoying the first rhubarb pie of the year early next March, I must start the process now. The old leaves of the spent crowns have died back completely, so I clean away all the debris, fork the soil over lightly, and then give the bed a liberal dose of very old manure.

Many connoisseurs of forced rhubarb advise leaving the crowns alone until February, but not me! I cover a selected crown – which is one that has not been forced for at least three years – with an old plastic dustbin, anchored down well with large bricks so that it does not go blowing away in the winter winds. And there you have the perfect microclimate for

Crown of rhubarb ready for dividing

growth, encouraging the crown in the New Year to send up its tender, pale pink stalks in search of the excluded light. I am licking my lips already at the thought of what is to come!

Rhubarb might be reliable and bone hardy, but even this old warrior needs some maintenance from time to time. After six or seven years the bulk of the crown gets very woody, and now is a good time to lift the whole crown and give it some severe surgery, cutting off and releasing a young portion with a new bud from the old fibrous remains. To stimulate growth leave the new part on the surface of the soil for a good frosting. Prepare a fresh bed for it with plenty of bulky compost (see page 23), and replant the young crown in late January. Then look out in years to come for lots of tender stalks to meet your culinary needs, with plenty more to give to family and friends.

Cleaning the pond

Many years ago I created a pond at the bottom of my plot by sinking a plastic bin in the soil, and since then I have been rewarded every February as this becomes the breeding ground for the local frog population, always welcome on my plot as my 'pest destroyers'.

At this time of year I tidy the area around the pond, safe in the knowledge that the frogs are tucked up in hibernation. During the spring and summer I allow tall grasses and nettles to colonize the bank all round the pond so that these amphibians can leave the water out of sight of the local birds that populate the hedge at the bottom of my plot. It is also a great sanctuary for the young froglets as they emerge in the early summer and feast on the aphids that I feed them. Should a straying hedgehog fall in, there is even a platform in the pond so that it can emerge safely. I need all the friends I can get as an organic gardener!

Quick leafmould

An ever-increasing stock of leaves can mean having to make an extra wire compound to house them. Ideally I need to accelerate their breakdown so that the leafmould is ready in late spring for adding to some of my beds. I have no need to use the liquid produced by my wormery as a plant feed at this time of year, so this goes into my watering can in a strong dilution to make a superb activator, with which I thoroughly douse the leaves. They are then covered with plastic bags, anchored down with strong metal posts, and as more wormery liquid becomes available it is added to the heap. Hopefully by spring there will be plenty of rich fresh leafmould to add to my seed beds.

Time to coppice raspberries

My late-fruiting raspberries, 'Autumn Bliss', are a great investment, with a long fruiting period that often extends into October if the weather is favourable. This 'end of term' variety gives some of the best soft fruits of the year, which add something a bit special to those dessert dishes before the onset of winter, topping up my vitamin C levels to ward off winter sniffles.

Alas, they are no more – the first frosts finish their season – and to ensure another bumper crop next year all the branches that have borne these fruits must be given the chop. They are all cut off at ground level and left to dry out for burning later in the winter, producing valuable potash to be returned to the base of the plants to boost their next fruit crop. Clean up around the base of the plants, cover the ground with a liberal dose of well-rotted manure, and the dormant plants can be left to restore their vigour for next year's performance.

Conquering canker

The large blue bins that were home to some of my carrots are exhausted now, so they can be emptied and then restocked with my home-made compost ready to house some of next year's parsnips. I always add a generous supply of horticultural sand to improve drainage, plus a sprinkling of lime to make the final mix slightly alkaline, in the hope this will reduce the chance of canker attacking the long roots.

Parsnips are one of the earliest sowings of the year, so this preparation is necessary now to allow the bins to settle; then I can see if they need topping up with more compost before planting time in late March. Parsnips seem to be a feature of my allotment life the whole year around, because the new year's crop is sown and growing before I have completed harvesting the old. In fact the parsnip is almost a perpetual vegetable on my plot!

Parsnip seedlings planted in drum

Looking back

Stocking up on my autumn supply of manure sent my ageing mind racing back to my youthful days of the 1950s on this very allotment.

As a teenager one of my summer tasks was to gather bracken from the hillside during August, just when it was at its nutritional best to enhance the fertility of what was then my father's allotment. All through the long summer school holidays I could be found deep in this bracken, wielding my little scythe – hours of 'cut and slash' would produce a huge mound of chopped greenery. Then came the lengthy task of pitchforking this mound down the hillside to my father's plot. Hour by hour the heap would grow into a very large stack, and I would step back and admire the results of my labour.

Imagine my disappointment as a youth, watching this mound shrink daily throughout the winter months until by the following spring it was only about one-tenth of the volume I'd collected. It was a fabulous organic soil improver, though, especially when supplemented by horse manure from the local colliery stables. Back in the 1950s coal was brought from the face by ponies, and every colliery yard had a stables. They were glad to dispose of this by-product, and local allotments were grateful recipients.

Who says 'organic' is a recent gardening phenomenon? Back in my youth it was the only way.

NOVEMBER IN A NUTSHELL

Key jobs for NOVEMBER

✔ Keep a close eye on leeks for rust; also watch for signs of bolting, quickly harvesting those affected.

✔ Insulate the inside of the greenhouse with bubble wrap to keep its inhabitants a degree or two warmer.

✔ Prepare the greenhouse border for next year's crops.

✔ Collect any late falls of leaves and compost them in a wire frame for more lovely leafmould.

If you have time . . .

✔ Repair or make new frames to support the mesh to enclose next year's maincrop carrots.

Looking ahead to DECEMBER

✔ Start filling pots with good compost to warm up in the greenhouse for some early sowings of broad beans.

✔ Harvest the first carrots from a summer-sown drum that has flourished in the greenhouse.

✔ Study the seed catalogues to order next year's seeds for planned crops.

✔ Fill some large pots with good compost and sow early salad crops in the greenhouse.

✔ Check stored potatoes for any rodents that may have invaded the shed.

Thought for the month

November is a time for contemplation on the plot. No, this is not some new strange type of crop, but a chance at the end of another growing year to look forward to the next.

I find that gardeners very rarely dwell for long on the past, and are forever looking to the future – I suppose this is what makes us such an optimistic lot. After all, you cannot change the past, but if you plan ahead according to what has gone before, your choice of action may have more effect in the future. My dad always said you learn from your mistakes, and then move forward to bigger and better things. Nowhere is this truer, I find, than on the allotments.

Frosty allotment

DECEMBER

THERE IS GOOD REASON TO BE JOLLY this month: 21 December signals the shortest day. Soon the hours of daylight will be extending and we will be marching into a new exciting year.

When I open the morning curtains I gaze out on scenes that look as if they have been dusted by a large salt cellar: white frost glistens under the azure skies, giving that view often found on Christmas cards. The sun may be a late riser at this time of year but, boy, is it worth waiting for!

This is the start of the festive season, so there's more time to spend with the family and even passionate gardeners like me enjoy the short shopping excursions. The dark days and diminishing tasks on the plot relieve any guilt I might feel at leaving it alone for a couple of days.

If the weather is unkind, there is always planning to be done. Those brightly coloured seed packets have arrived, so I can sit by the fireside and work out where they all are to go in the springtime, bringing forth great dreams and expectation of the next season in the comfort of my armchair. There's still good reason to go down to the plot, though, where there is plenty to be done in the warmer climes under glass. My belief is that an hour spent now saves five in the spring.

The days when you do manage to get down to the plot bring cheer to your very soul. And then, what can be better after a visit there than to get home to a mug of steaming coffee and a hot mince pie? This gets the festive spirit under way and helps make those December days a much more pleasurable experience.

Look carefully this month and you will find new life appearing already on the patches of bare soil before winter tightens its icy grip. You might see the little green shoots of those winter onions, while close examination could reveal the camouflaged tips of the garlic.

Don't grow too quickly, though, my little ones, or the harsh conditions of the next two months may give you a severe shock! There is plenty still to do below ground where it is warmer: the forming of a strong root structure so that your energies will be put to good use sending up your strong green growth when the days lengthen and turn milder.

Life is everywhere

It is not just on Christmas cards that we see the robin. During our forays into the garden our red-breasted ally is usually chasing us around in the hope that we will unearth some tasty morsels to help him weather the cold and winter hunger.

The robin is not the only feathered friend that stays at home during these winter days, rather than flying off to warmer climes. Decking out the garden with a range of bird feeders stuffed with peanuts, wild bird seed, nyger seeds and fat balls will encourage a whole host of colourful birds that will brighten these drab days and bring hours of pleasure – much better than television, creating your own *Winter Watch* before your very eyes.

On the dullest of days the bright green and yellow plumes of the blue tit will be seen as it feeds away. Then there are the grandly coloured members of the finch family: chaffinches, the goldfinch with his red and white mask, the bright yellows and greens of the greenfinch, and the rosy pink face and breast of the bullfinch. These delightful dressy visitors to our gardens replace the splendour of showy summer annual flowers that are long gone.

Then there are the sombre colours of the starlings with their mottled breasts and amusing antics, and the jet black of a male blackbird rooting among the debris for a morsel or two. There, darting furtively among the winter remnants of summer plants, moves the secretive jenny wren, while sparrows chirp away merrily in the denser evergreen shrubs. I'm particularly pleased to see the gardener's best ally, the song thrush, back in residence.

All these wonderful creatures are very welcome in my garden. As a gardener I feel it is my duty to work in harmony with nature's creatures (well almost: slugs and snails excepted, of course). Their habitats are fragile, under constant threat from intensive farming and the indiscriminate use of pesticides, but by creating our own little havens we can partly help redress this situation for the benefit of all. It is a sorry garden that lacks the cheerful chorus and diverse behaviour of some of nature's most delightful creatures.

My seeds are here!

My seed order has arrived, the best Christmas present of all, and my excitement is growing! This is a job for a warm comfortable place indoors, where they are unpacked, inspected, and then sorted into order to help my ageing brain remember what to sow and when.

Never worry about the sowing dates shown on seed packets – these are just a rough guide, and it is more realistic to use your own judgement according to the prevailing weather. It is better to be a little late than to rush them in while temperatures are still too cold. Temperature is a key factor in getting seeds to germinate, and if they are too cold there is a high likelihood of complete failure, with a whole packet of seeds going to waste.

Good-quality compost is also essential for seed germination, so buy a decent bag of it and do not skimp on cost or again the seed will be lost. The final condition for successful germination is water: too much and they will rot, but just right and they will grow.

Tales from the plot

The days are still getting shorter, and those few hours of daylight that are available are often very dingy and unappealing. The up-side of December, however, is that the festive season is nearly with us, and even dedicated allotmenteers love the fun of Christmas. There may not be many carol singers at the allotment gates, but Albie's café is decked out cheerfully.

Occasionally I get the chance to stroll through the allotments looking at the contrast between all the various plots. Two (Carl's and Terry S's) always stand out during the winter months because they are dug over from top to bottom, with the soil left rough in large clods for the weather to pulverize into a fine tilth by the spring. These large expanses of well-tended ground look pristine and very neat with an even finish and not a weed in sight.

Another memorable sight one year was on Kevin's plot. There, sheltered in the corner, were the remnants of his summer sweet peas, and – much to everyone's amazement – these were still flowering, despite a few heavy frosts. It's these little bright spots that lift the spirits on dull days and cheer you up, even in the depths of winter.

I had a shock the other morning when I opened my shed door. Piled up against the back of the door was a loose heap of dried organic manure, below a massive ragged hole in the bag. There was no doubt about the cause: Mr Rat had taken up residence, and I had a new lodger!

There was only one answer to this intrusion and that was eviction, but first of all I had to find out how it got in. As I know from experience it takes hours to empty the shed of all my worldly possessions – I am constantly amazed how it all fits into this small space – but eventually I found in the back corner a small hole in the floorboard, recently and carefully nibbled through. Much hammering and banging ensued. Finally a new board was in place, with fervent hopes that, once expelled, the unwanted lodger would get the message and stay out.

Anthony, one of our newer members, arrived one morning recently and gazed in astonishment at the shredded remains of his polytunnel. He was warned about the ferocity of the winds that blow on this hillside and has paid the price – just one small hole left unrepaired in the plastic sheet, and our wind will tear it to pieces. On the bright side, the shreds and strips of torn plastic act as great bird scarers! However, he was straight on to the case with thicker plastic anchored down more securely. You cannot keep a keen gardener down.

Meanwhile the rest of us were having our annual get-together in Albie's abode before the seasonal few days' break from the allotments. Brian, Nuts, Keith, Albie and I were sharing a bottle or two of wine to celebrate another good year on the plots, finishing off the party with a couple of carols for good measure – the acoustics in Albie's greenhouse are almost as good as in the Albert Hall!

If you fancy sharing the festive fun, please join in with my home-grown carol:

Good old Albie, he looked out while making coffee creamy,
Watching Brian working there, barrowing manure so steamy.
Sun shone brightly o'er the plots, though the frost was cruel,
When Terry came into sight, gathering veg for gruel.

'Hither, Nuts, come stand by me. Who's that bloke that's yelling?
Yonder gardener, who is he? Where and what's his dwelling?'
'Terry, he lives a long way hence, underneath that mountain,
Right against the allotment fence by the stream and fountain.'

'Boys, the sky is darker now and the wind blows stronger.
I am feeling colder now, and I can stay no longer!'
So in Terry's footsteps they went forth together,
Through the cold wind's wild lament and the bitter weather.

On my way to the allotment one morning I noticed part of the road was up, with engineers at work replacing underground telephone wires. The wires are channelled through plastic ducts, and a heap of offcuts of this tubing lay to one side.

The inventive eye of the experienced allotmenteer looked, and immediately a use came to mind, so I asked if I could have them and they were gladly handed over. Cut into lengths of about 6 inches (15 cm) they made perfect blanching tubes for my leeks, which I can reuse year after year.

This was not the only useful dumped gift I came across that day. An old enamel washing bowl I spotted on a skip was soon winging its way to my greenhouse, its size a perfect fit beneath my sieve to make the job of sifting compost much easier. It takes years of practice, though, to find a use for every kind of reusable throwaway!

Every year I hope and pray it will not snow before Christmas Eve, otherwise Christmas dinner in our house would be a disaster, for that is the day when I visit the plot to collect all the vegetables I need to grace the feast in the Walton household. There must be parsnips, sweeter after all the autumn frosts than

they ever are earlier in the year. We need Brussels sprouts as green and firm as golf balls, swedes to purée with fresh cream, and those long, slender leeks for braising alongside our traditional turkey. The hidden sacks of potatoes in the store shed will be holding all that nourishment locked into them during the summer months. Hanging from the shed rafters are the brown, shiny orbs of my onions beside a bunch of dried leaves that might look unappetizing but when crushed release the spicy fragrance of sage.

Harvesting winter veg

Laden with my allotment booty I return home like the original hunter-gatherer. This is one of the few times of the year when I am let loose in the kitchen with a sharp knife to clean all these vegetables, while my wife Anthea gets to work making the stuffing and preparing the turkey. With the sound of carols ringing around the kitchen, glasses of sherry in hand, the ambience is complete. We are both in full festive mode.

It's around now that I am most aware how fragile my claim for self-sufficiency can be.

It has always been my goal to live off my plot all year round, and each year I get a little closer to realizing that ambition. Many people ask me the secrets of a constant supply of home-grown produce, but there are none. It is all about sensitive soil management and careful planning – crop rotation to avoid pests and diseases if you grow organically; enriching the soil with the correct nutrients and plenty of manures in the appropriate places; composting to replace what you take out of the ground and to stimulate those good micro-organisms in the soil; lime for the brassica family; and plenty of beans and peas to enrich the soil with the nitrogen they store in their roots.

The important part of having good fertility in your patch is that rich soil can support more than one crop per season, and it is this kind of heavy cropping that's necessary if you are to live largely off the land. As every crop is harvested, another must follow, at the least a simple catch crop that has a speedy life cycle from sowing to plate, which can therefore slip in without compromising the planned crop rotation sequence.

Sometimes it seems to me as if, to get the plants of our choice to grow, we are having to fight nature, whereas weeds pop up and flourish effortlessly. These are nature's survivors, and I often wonder why we do not just eat the weeds and give up growing the cultivated crops. But it is this annual battle to grow just what we want, and in the place of our choice, that makes gardening such a challenging and irresistible hobby. The rewards when we sit down to a feast of fresh tasty vegetables make it all worthwhile.

IN THE GREENHOUSE

On days when the ground remains out of bounds, too wet or frozen for me to do anything useful outside, it always pays to get ahead of the game under glass. Used polystyrene cups, already cleaned and equipped with drainage holes burned in the base, are ready to be filled to house my broad beans. These are big plants, even in the infant stage, and I find they need a good compost to sustain them over the weeks prior to planting out in late March. I mix one part wormery compost with three parts multi-purpose compost, fill the cups with this rich mixture, and then store them in plastic mushroom trays (each conveniently holds twenty cups) under the staging to warm up.

All my seed trays and pots must be clean and disease-free for the first sowings in the heated greenhouse in January (not that far away!). I wash them thoroughly in a bucket of warm water to which I have added a little disinfectant, then leave them to dry on the staging ready for use in a few weeks' time. Old plant labels are treated similarly: a bowl of warm soapy water, a little piece of fine sandpaper, and last year's writing is soon removed.

By now there is usually a pile of dirty plastic tubes that I have stripped from the perfect white shanks of my harvested leeks. To make sure no rust spores are carried over from infected plants to next year's crop, I scrub these tubes clean, using disinfectant and a stiff bottle brush to remove any lingering disease, and store them away in pristine condition.

The first of many sowings

I try to leave the festivities for an hour, with a packet of onion seeds in hand, and escape to the peace and solitude of my greenhouse. Sets are by far and away the simplest way to grow onions, but if you like a challenge you cannot beat growing a few monster specimens from seed.

They are not difficult to grow but do require a long season to reach a good size, and soon after the shortest day is the time to start them off. I fill a

Onion seedlings

seed tray with good seed compost, disperse the jet-black seeds evenly over the surface, lightly cover them with the same sieved compost, and then firm them gently. A spray of tepid water to moisten the compost, and then they go in the greenhouse, where they should pop through the surface after about two weeks spent in a temperature of 12–5 °C.

Too high a temperature has an adverse effect on germination, so I erect a 'mini-greenhouse' inside my greenhouse, and use a paraffin lamp to supply just enough gentle heat to create a perfect propagating area. A small hand sprayer filled with tepid water keeps the seeds evenly moist without the risk of overwatering.

And so we are off with this first step towards another exciting sowing season. Soon the greenhouse will be bulging with new arrivals once more!

DECEMBER TASKS

'Whatever do you find to do on that plot of yours at this time of year?' my wife asks almost daily during December.

To which I reply, 'Well, my love, there is always something to do when you have an allotment.'

And that's how it is for most people: tending an allotment is not just for summer, it's a full year's commitment.

Getting ready for New Year

If the weather is favourable I can get ahead with some early preparation on the plot to save time when the new season's pace hots up. The manure that I stack during the summer is usually in perfect condition around now, and has served its purpose of feeding my local robin throughout the cold days.

Spreading manure

Cutting pea sticks

Now I am eager to get it spread on the plot, particularly on the areas where my broad beans and potatoes will be planted. A very frosty morning would be ideal for trundling my barrow across the soil without damaging its structure. With the well-rotted manure spread thickly, I can then leave it for a few weeks before digging it in to produce the super-fertile ground these crops thrive in.

Then there's the hedge at the bottom of my plot. It makes a great backdrop but tends to send up too many overhanging branches that create a great deal of shade – most vegetables are basically sun-loving and do not thrive in the shade. Extended loppers are just the tool for tackling these long, spindly branches. It does not take long before the trees are shaped up, leaving my plot able to bask in full light again.

The large bundle of prunings I am left with are put to good use, the thinner branches snipped up with the aid of my secateurs to produce a pile of pea sticks ready to support next year's rambling peas, while the heap of thick main boughs that remains will soon be burned in my brazier to make some good wood ash.

While trying to suppress my growing anticipation of the new season ahead, I like to make time over Christmas to review the past year, its successes or failures, and in particular the vegetable varieties I have grown. Sometimes these have arrived as packets on the front of gardening magazines, an excellent way to discover and try something new! These are typical notes from my allotment records.

One of my finds of the year was 'Valdor' lettuce. For many years I grew 'Fortune', which suited both early and late sowings, but when it disappeared off the market I was left in the wilderness until 'Valdor' appeared. When this was sown in early February in the greenhouse and planted out under a cloche in March, I had my early lettuce back under control. Sown in late summer, it gave me my last outdoor crop during early autumn, while a September sowing gave me leafy salad under glass in time

Organizing seeds and sowing 'Primo' cabbage

for Christmas. It fared well in extreme weather, with no sign of bolting or fungal diseases, and a single packet was sufficient for the whole growing season when sown indoors in small amounts. That's value for money!

'White Lisbon' spring onions were perfect for adding crunch and flavour to my salads. A first sowing in February in a florist's bucket in the greenhouse was ready with the first lettuces. I never sow spring onions directly into the soil, and instead sow a fresh bucket every three weeks throughout the season to produce a constant supply almost year-round. The only lean period was during February and March, so that needs a little more planning.

Along came March, and with it a free packet of 'Boltardy' beetroot. These are never sown direct, but started in twenty small pots, two seeds per potful of good compost. The unthinned seedlings are planted out after just a few weeks, then the first are pulled when they are as large as golf balls and the rest left to reach tennis-ball size. Sown at three-weekly intervals, the single packet produced a year-long supply.

Also in March there were free packets of 'Gardener's' Delight' cherry tomatoes and 'World Beater' peppers. The tomatoes (plenty of plants to give away from one packet) are great, giving an early picking of small tomatoes and a very heavy crop over the whole season with less fuss than standard-size varieties and no need to remove sideshoots. They do well outdoors but are less prone to blight under cover, where they crop early and go on well into autumn. The peppers, however, tested my patience to the extreme: despite an early sowing it was a long time to the first harvest.

'Musselburgh' is still a good all-round variety of the vegetable close to every Welshman's heart, the leek. They need a long season (but continue cropping right into the autumn and winter), so need starting in half-size seed trays during late March for planting out in late April, in holes made with a crowbar. I feed them regularly, and when they are tall enough wrap the stems in collars to ensure at least 9 inches (23 cm) of perfect white blanch.

'Primo' cabbage is a variety for all seasons. Sown in small amounts at four-week intervals in seed trays and grown on into decent plants before planting out, this supplied greens all spring, summer and autumn, holding well without bolting. The first crop was ready in May after planting out under cloches to accelerate growth. One packet saved a fortune in bought cabbages, with just a net to protect them from munching caterpillars and an occasional feed from my organic fertilizer repertoire.

Along came April and a new courgette to try, 'Nano Verde di Milano'. Seeds are started in 3-inch (8 cm) pots and moved on into larger containers until all danger of frosts has passed. Once planted out they romp away, first providing a gentle supply of tender green fruits – but then, as the season progresses, they throw them out in sackfuls! Courgette seeds should come with a warning! As the summer nights become humid, so mildew may take hold, but a spray of one part milk to ten parts water can help neutralize the attack.

I am a lover of runner beans, but in recent years I have become a convert to French beans, particularly climbing varieties like 'Climbing Blue Lake', a useful bean that seems to weather a wet Welsh summer and supply daily pickings, swelling the freezer stocks as well as gracing the dinner plate. To me, French beans taste much better than runner beans when frozen, and will guarantee a taste of summer in the depths of winter.

Love them or loathe them, swedes such as 'Invitation' are my winter favourite, an under-rated vegetable that helps supply the backbone of my winter cropping regime. Sown in compartmental seed trays in mid-May to avoid mildew taking hold, they are transplanted outside in mid-June and grow on to make a large amount of green topgrowth (popular with the cabbage white butterflies!) before transferring all this 'green energy' into purple swollen roots that keep me satisfied until the end of the following April.

One of my greatest finds was the lettuce 'Red Iceberg', a colourful tight 'crisp' variety with the distinction of holding well and not running to seed. It was a real discovery for me, the kind that regularly pops up even after a lifetime of gardening and makes my hobby truly worthwhile. One packet, a whole summer and autumn of good tasty lettuce – what more can I ask?

Looking back

I learned most of my early gardening skills from my father, who had a plot on this site for many years. For example, he taught me one sure-fire method of giving your seeds a good chance to germinate. I was shown how to lay the palm of my hand on the soil prior to sowing: if I felt a cold shiver I had to leave the seeds in the packet. When the soil feels warm and moist to my tender touch, then those small seeds will have a comfortable home and a good start in life. There is a lot we can take on board from gardeners of the past, and I always advise newcomers to look to the 'old hands' on the allotment for tips that should never be lost.

Another thing my father did was to disappear on Christmas morning after breakfast to collect all his fresh vegetables, but that's one practice I have changed because I am sworn to stay at home on this family day. If I were to go to the allotments on Christmas morn, there's no telling when Christmas lunch would finally be served, so I sacrifice those sixteen hours of extra freshness for the sake of peace and goodwill – it is meant to be a family-friendly time, after all!

Something that doesn't change, though, is the delight of seeing a contented group of family members sitting around the table with their plates wiped clean, and knowing that all those vegetables I nurtured from as far back as last spring have been enjoyed with such delight. This is thanks enough for the love and care expended on the plot throughout their long growing life. The true art of gardening is providing good food most of the year round.

If you have never grown winter vegetables before, give them a try, and you too could experience the pleasures of your own home-grown Christmas dinner. Go on, give it a go!

DECEMBER IN A NUTSHELL

Key jobs for DECEMBER

✔ Sow onion seeds for super-size onions.

✔ Sort out newly arrived seed packets into approximate sowing dates.

✔ Cut back overgrown hedges and get a free supply of pea sticks.

✔ Fill pots ready in the greenhouse for early broad bean sowings.

If you have time . . .

✔ When the ground is hard and frozen spread manure where greedy crops like beans and potatoes are to grow.

Looking ahead to JANUARY

✔ Buy seed potatoes and get them ready for chitting.

✔ Dig in those patches of green manure when ground is workable.

✔ Prepare sweet pea bed with plenty of good soil improvers.

✔ Lime areas ready for brassicas.

✔ Sow lettuce and cabbage in a warm greenhouse for those early spring crops.

✔ Sow sweet peas and broad beans in a warm spot.

Winter veg

Thought for the month

One of the joys of clear frosty nights this month is the chance to step out into the night and admire and wonder at that beautiful night sky, filled with thousands of glittering diamonds and, much larger than the rest, the moon bathing the land in pure white light.

Some gardeners maintain the moon controls their very actions, and they grow their crops biodynamically according to the lunar cycle. It is said that the new moon enhances root and shoot growth; the waxing moon rests roots while shoots grow; at full moon the roots grow whilst foliage rests; and during a waning moon both roots and shoots take a rest.

As I understand it, seed sowing is carried out two days before a new moon, as the next seven days are more favourable for germination, while the seven days following a full moon are the best time to transplant seedlings as their roots grow more strongly. Personally, I prefer to study temperature and moisture levels, and use my experience when deciding the best time to grow: if the soil is damp and warm, then those tiny seeds have the perfect conditions for starting life.

I do believe, however, that both lunar and organic practitioners have a deep understanding of how to keep the soil alive, and concentrate on the most vital part of success, which is building up and maintaining a stable, well-conditioned growing environment. The healthier the soil, the greater its ability to sustain plant growth and repel pests and diseases; and my firm belief is that soil nurtured using organic methods is healthier than ground subjected to the quick-fix chemical treatment. Never mind which method of gardening you choose, however odd it seems: it's the results and successes that count. If it works for you, why change?

INDEX

AUTHOR'S ACKNOWLEDGEMENTS

To all my family, who have been very supportive on my allotments and who have allowed me to indulge 'too many' hours there – sometimes at the expense of family life.

To Alun Owen and Susanna Wadeson at Transworld/Random House for encouraging me to pass on my allotment knowledge and share my many happy tales of life on the plot!

To all those allotmenteers past and present who provide the rich vein of stories and tips that forms the content of this book.

To Andi Clevely for his tireless support in making this book possible and for driving me on when the going got tough!

Terry Walton was born in 1946 in the Rhondda, and has lived in South Wales all his life. At the age of four he began to help out on his father's allotment, taking a plot of his own when he was eleven. He has gardened on the same allotment ever since. Terry's 'working life' was spent for the most part with a local company, where he became managing director. When he retired he was able to focus on his allotment, where he was discovered by Radio 2's *Jeremy Vine* show team. Terry gives updates live from his hillside plot every fortnight. He is also on the *Louise Elliot* show on BBC Wales Radio once a month in studio, BBC Radio Hereford & Worcester once a month live from the allotment, and makes appearances on Channel 4 *Super Scrimpers* to give his gardening tips. Terry has written articles for *Saga* online and for a variety of publications, including the *South Wales Echo* and *Garden News*.

TRANSWORLD PUBLISHERS
61–63 Uxbridge Road, London W5 5SA
A Random House Group Company
www.transworldbooks.co.uk

First published in Great Britain
in 2013 by Bantam Press
an imprint of Transworld Publishers

A CIP catalogue record for this book
is available from the British Library.

ISBN 9780593070697

Addresses for Random House Group Ltd companies outside the UK
can be found at: www.randomhouse.co.uk
The Random House Group Ltd Reg. No. 954009

Design: Isobel Gillan
Photography: Terry Walton

Typeset in Berkeley Old Style and Gill Sans
Printed and bound by
Toppan Leefung Printing Ltd, China

2 4 6 8 10 9 7 5 3 1